A LIFEBUILDER

J O B

Wrestling with God

*12 Studies
for individuals or groups*

Paul Stevens

With Notes for Leaders

SCRIPTURE UNION
207–209 QUEENSWAY, BLETCHLEY
MILTON KEYNES, BUCKINGHAMSHIRE (UK), MK2 2EB

GW00341208

© 1995 by R. Paul Stevens

First published in the United States by InterVarsity Press.
First published in Great Britain by Scripture Union, 1995.

All rights reserved. No part of this book may be reproduced, stored in a retrieval system, or transmitted, in any form
or by any means, electronic, mechanical, photocopying, recording or otherwise, without the prior permission
of Scripture Union.

Unless otherwise indicated, Scripture quotations are taken from the HOLY BIBLE, NEW INTERNATIONAL VERSION.
Copyright © 1973, 1978, 1984 by International Bible Society. Anglicisation copyright © 1979, 1984, 1989.
Used by permission of Hodder and Stoughton Limited.

Cover photograph: Dennis Frates

ISBN 0 86201 997 4

Printed in England by Ebenezer Baylis & Son Limited, The Trinity Press, Worcester and London

Contents

Getting the Most
from LifeBuilder Bible Studies

Many of us long to fill our minds and our lives with Scripture. We desire to be transformed by its message. LifeBuilder Bible Studies are designed to be an exciting and challenging way to do just that. Their ultimate goal is to help us build our lives on God's Word.

How They Work

LifeBuilder Bible Studies have a number of distinctive features. Perhaps the most important is that they are *inductive* rather than *deductive*. In other words, they lead us to *discover* what the Bible says rather than simply *telling* us what it says.

They are also thought provoking. They help us to think about the meaning of the passage so that we can truly understand what the author is saying. The questions require more than one-word answers.

The studies are personal. Questions expose us to the promises, assurances, exhortations and challenges of God's Word. They are designed to allow the Scriptures to renew our minds so that we can be transformed by the Spirit of God. This is the ultimate goal of all Bible study.

The studies are versatile. They are designed for student, neighbourhood and church groups. They are also effective for individual study.

How They're Put Together

LifeBuilder Bible Studies also have a distinctive format. Each study need take no more than forty-five minutes in a group setting or thirty minutes in a personal study – unless you choose to take more time.

The studies can be used within a quarter system in a church and fit well in a semester or trimester system on a college campus. If a guide has more than thirteen studies, it is divided into two or occasionally three parts of approximately twelve studies each.

LifeBuilder Bible Studies use a workbook format. Space is provided for writing answers to each question. This is ideal for personal study and allows group members to prepare in advance for the discussion.

The studies also contain leader's notes. They show how to lead a group discussion, provide additional background information on certain questions, give helpful tips on group dynamics and suggest ways to deal with problems which may arise during the discussion. With such helps, someone with little or no experience can lead an effective study.

Suggestions for Individual Study

1. As you begin each study, pray that God will help you to understand and apply the passage to your life.

2. Read and reread the assigned Bible passage to familiarize yourself with what the author is saying. In the case of book studies, you may want to read through the entire book prior to the first study. This will give you a helpful overview of its contents.

3. A good modern translation of the Bible, rather than the King James Version or a paraphrase, will give you the most help. The New International Version, the New American Standard Bible and the Revised Standard Version are all recommended. However, the questions in this guide are based on the New International Version.

4. Write your answers in the space provided in the study guide. This will help you to express your understanding of the passage clearly.

5. It might be good to have a Bible dictionary handy. Use it to look up any unfamiliar words, names or places.

Suggestions for Group Study

1. Come to the study prepared. Follow the suggestions for individual study mentioned above. You will find that careful preparation will greatly enrich your time spent in group discussion.

2. Be willing to participate in the discussion. The leader of your group will not be lecturing. Instead, he or she will be encouraging the members of the group to discuss what they have learned from the passage. The leader will be asking the questions that are found in this guide. Plan to share what God has taught you in your individual study.

3. Stick to the passage being studied. Your answers should be based on the verses which are the focus of the discussion and not on outside authorities such as commentaries or speakers. This guide deliberately avoids jumping

from book to book or passage to passage. Each study focuses on only one passage. Book studies are generally designed to lead you through the book in the order in which it was written. This will help you follow the author's argument.

4. Be sensitive to the other members of the group. Listen attentively when they share what they have learned. You may be surprised by their insights! Link what you say to the comments of others so the group stays on the topic. Also, be affirming whenever you can. This will encourage some of the more hesitant members of the group to participate.

5. Be careful not to dominate the discussion. We are sometimes so eager to share what we have learned that we leave too little opportunity for others to respond. By all means participate! But allow others to also.

6. Expect God to teach you through the passage being discussed and through the other members of the group. Pray that you will have an enjoyable and profitable time together.

7. If you are the discussion leader, you will find additional suggestions and helpful ideas for each study in the leader's notes. These are found at the back of the guide.

Introducing Job

"The malady of our time lies in its contracted thoughts of God."[1]

One thing we can count on in this life is *trouble!* Becoming a Christian, contrary to what some say, does not so much deliver us from problems as deliver us *in* them. We still get sick, lose jobs, worry about our children and struggle with loneliness. On a deeper level a personal encounter with God brings at the same time exquisite joy and a new set of questions. Sometimes, like Job, we are led through a dark valley without seeing the path out, why we are suffering, whether God has a redeeming purpose in it all and how we are to respond. Are we to just patiently take it all?

Mention the name *Job* and one immediately thinks of patience, partly because of one misunderstood New Testament reference to this Old Testament saint (Jas 5:11). Job did suffer, but not patiently. He rebelled. Job's saintly friends tried to "explain" his problems by appealing to the logic of good orthodox theology. In the end, Job's almost irreverent appeal to God for an explanation led to his justification and approval by God. While Job's orthodox churchgoing friends were rejected (Job 42:7), he persevered; that is the real point of the New Testament reference. Perhaps, among other things, this surprising reversal can be explained by the fact that Job spoke *to* God about his suffering, while Job's friends spoke *about* God to Job. But this is not the only mystery encompassed by this fascinating Old Testament book.

The book of Job raises as many questions as its answers. Indeed, when God finally speaks to Job in the whirlwind (chapters 38—41), God himself asks questions! Traditionally theology has wrestled with how a good and all-powerful God could allow or even *cause* (as Job claims) suffering and evil in the world. Not only are the usual abstract arguments–spoken smoothly by Job's three friends, Eliphaz, Bildad and Zophar—rejected by God and his beloved Job; they are not even the point of the book.

This is not a book of rational, systematic theology. This is the story of one human being—one very human and very righteous being—who loses his possessions, his family and his health. But it is a story that takes place within the household of faith. And it is faith that rebels and a God who loves the rebel that is the surprise of the story.

In a closed universe (the view assumed by the ancient Greeks and modern secularized people) human beings are tragic victims of fate. In a dualistic universe where God and Satan are equal opponents in the battle of good and evil, one can blame all adversity on the devil. But in the book of Job, as elsewhere in the Bible, God shares his ultimate sovereignty with no one, not even Satan.[2]

Job—and we—have problems with innocent suffering precisely because we have faith in God, whose goodness is known in the land of the living. There is no answer either in jettisoning belief in the goodness of God or in rejecting the hope that *in this life* there should be both satisfaction and justice. In the end, *and only in the end,* Job finds peace with God through his sufferings, and not in spite of them. Ultimately, Job's passion points to the death, resurrection and vindication of Jesus as God's final answer to the problem of the innocent suffering.

The gospel-bearing quality of Job is all the more remarkable because the book may be very ancient. There is no mention of temple, monarchy or prophets. We do not know who wrote the book, when or where the author lived, though there is no adequate reason to deny the unity of the book.[3]

The book contains an astonishing mixture of riddles, hymns, curses, proverbs and nature poems. The introduction (1:1—2:13) and conclusion (42:7-17) are in prose, while the speeches of Job, the three friends, the young man Elihu and God himself (3:1—42:6) are in poetry. No wonder the Jewish rabbis were unsure where to place Job in Scripture. Though they eventually chose the "writings" section, this book fits just as well alongside the great exodus, David and Ruth.

Like all biblical stories, this one catches us in its plot and invites us in its mysterious and ironic way to find God, not in talking *about* God, but in talking *to* him, not in the familiar rhythms of safe theological discussion, but at the point of our deepest questions about the meaning of life and of God himself, not in leisure-time spirituality, but in the middle of life where it is hardest. "The book takes its place in the testimony of the ages that there is a blank in the human heart which Jesus alone can fill."[4]

---

[1]D. S. Cairns, *The Faith That Rebels* (SCM Press, 1928).

[2]Francis I. Andersen, *Job: An Introduction and Commentary,* Tyndale Old Testament Commentaries (InterVarsity Press, 1976), pp. 34-35, 64-65.

For date, authorship and textual questions read ibid., pp. 15-76.

[4]F. Davidson, A. M. Stibbs and E. F. Kevan, eds., *The New Bible Commentary* (InterVarsity Press, 1953), p. 388.

1
Dueling with the Devil
Job 1:1—2:10

Is it possible to love God for God's sake, and not merely for the benefits of being faithful, even when there *are* benefits? And what if these benefits are all removed and one is left with no benefit but God alone?

The "upstairs—downstairs" drama of the book of Job starts with a contest, probably in heaven, between Satan, the Accuser, and God concerning the purity of Job's spirituality. God and Satan make an agreement, less like spiritual warfare and more like a duel—with honor at stake and equivalency of weapons. "Downstairs," in Job's world, our hero goes through the loss of everything *except* the ultimate treasure, and even that seems threatened.

1. How would you respond to someone who charges that religion is only for those who can't make it on their own?

2. Read Job 1:1-22. What indications are there that Job's righteousness was not directly related to his being blessed with material prosperity (vv. 1-8)?

3. In this very ancient document Satan appears as an angelic adversary with free access to God's presence, unlike the devil in the New Testament. What does Satan accuse Job of (vv. 9-11)?

4. For what good reasons could God agree to a contest that would affect Job and his family so painfully?

5. Though Job apparently is unaware of God's approval, what signs indicate that this is important for Job?

6. How does Job react to the first test (vv. 20-22)?

7. In what ways is Job's response different from responses people make today to life's hard blows?

8. As will be apparent later, Job's righteous response (v. 22) included questioning God about the apparent injustice of his situation. What could be sinful behavior in Job's reaction?

9. Read Job 2:1-10. Why do you think God agreed to this second test?

10. God did not allow Satan to take Job's life. The Adversary attacked Job's possessions, his family and his health. What further attack did Job sustain from his wife (vv. 9-10)?

Why would her suggestion be especially dangerous to Job's faith?

11. Suffering is a mystery, and the opening scenes of this book deepen the mystery by showing how inadequate are our "reasons" for misfortune. What have you already learned about "accepting trouble from God" (v. 10)?

What difference will this make to your own attitude toward hard times?

☐ Cynicism is the essence of the satanic. The Satan believes nothing to be genuinely good—neither Job in his disinterested piety nor God in His disinterested generosity. . . . Cynicism is studied disbelief; and a mind turned in upon its own malice is the final horror of the diabolical. **Francis Andersen**[1]

[1]Andersen, *Job*, p. 84.

2
God in the Dark

Job 2:11—4:17

For every ten people who can withstand the temptations of adversity, only one can stand prosperity—or so it is said. It was different with our Old Testament hero. Job has handled his prosperity as a ministry, and later defends his stewardship of abundance (29:7-25; 31:24-25). But now he is plunged into excruciating loss, a living death. This new test will examine whether his belief in the goodness of God can be subverted by unalterably negative circumstances. Job will ask questions that are asked in wars and famines, when people are faced with congenital deformities and terminal illnesses. Job will later take up the cause of all the nameless, suffering poor (24:1-25). But in this study Job feels the weight of his own burden first.

1. Describe an experience in which you were tempted to doubt God's goodness. (What questions did you ask? What thoughts, if any, did you have of God?)

2. At this point in the story Job's three friends travel a considerable distance to console Job. Read Job 2:11-13. What actions of the friends indicate they understood how deeply Job was suffering?

3. From chapters 3 through 31 the story moves from prose to poetry as Job's three friends discuss the meaning of his adversity and where—if anywhere—God was present in the darkness. Read Job 3:1-26. In what ways does Job's response to his suffering go beyond asking the usual why (vv. 1-10)?

4. Though Job curses his birthday (v. 1), he does not curse God. What is the difference?

5. What does Job think God's role is in all this (vv. 11, 16)?

6. What new questions does Job ask in verses 20-26?

7. In what ways does Job's speech go beyond the "poor me" complaint so frequently uttered by people in times of adversity?

8. Each of Job's three friends makes a speech with Job responding—a cycle that gets repeated three times in the book. Read Job 4:1-17. Eliphaz responds cautiously at first and then attacks. Why does Eliphaz think Job is suffering?

9. Eliphaz counsels, "Should not your piety be your confidence and your blameless ways your hope?" (4:6). Is this sound advice helpful? Explain.

10. Eliphaz thinks he has God's word (4:12-17). Job only has dark questions. What have you learned so far about finding God in the midst of pain and loss?

11. How do you feel about living with unanswered questions?

□ Talk to me about the truth of religion and I'll listen gladly. Talk to me about the duty of religion and I'll listen submissively. But don't come talking to me about the consolations of religion or I shall suspect that you don't understand. **C. S. Lewis**[1]

[1]*A Grief Observed* (Faber & Faber Limited, 1966), p. 23.

3
God-Talk:
How Not to Be
Spiritual Friends
Job 6

W ith friends like these, who needs enemies!" might well be Job's heart-cry, and sometimes our own.

Even our worst experiences of friendship do not quench our desire for soul friends, people who will walk with us through life's hardest moments and who will point us to God without preaching at us or judging our spirituality. Most of us are lonely, as was our Old Testament hero.

"Job's comforters" is the cynical title given to Eliphaz, Bildad and Zophar—and later the young man Elihu. But they started well. Hearing about their friend's disaster, they came to him, wept, sat with him in silence (2:11-13). Unfortunately, the rest of the story is less exemplary, as we shall soon see. Sometimes people are presented in the Bible—often without editorial comment—simply to show us what *not* to do!

1. Reflect on the friend who has been most encouraging in your spiritual journey. Use single words to characterize your relationship with that person.

2. In the last study we discovered that Eliphaz's approach to Job was "you are suffering because of your sin or your children's sin." Review Eliphaz's attempt to comfort Job (4:1—5:27). Why were Eliphaz's words so unhelpful?

3. Read Job 6:1-21. Instead of responding to Eliphaz's accusation, Job explores his problem on a deeper level. For what new reason does he want God to end it all (v. 10)?

4. What word pictures does Job use to describe his friends (vv. 15-21)?

What do these metaphors mean?

5. Do you agree with Job that "a despairing man should have the devotion of his friends, even though he forsakes the fear of the Almighty" (v. 14)? Why or why not?

6. Is it always right to maintain a friendship even if your friend "loses" faith or goes through a period of rebellion?

7. What reason does Job see underlying his friends' failure to minister to him (v. 21)?

8. What does Job need from his friends in this time of suffering?

Why are his friends apparently unable to help him?

9. Later Job will comment, "Men at ease have contempt for misfortune" (12:5). What would enable you to be of help to others in the pit of despair even though you are doing fine yourself?

10. Read Job 6:22-30. How could Job's friends have confidence in his integrity (v. 29) even though they have no explanation for his problem except God's discipline?

11. What have you learned about how *not* to be a friend?

how to be a friend?

☐ A true friend can never have a hidden motive for being a friend. He can have no hidden agenda. A friend is simply a friend, for the sake of friendship. In a much greater way, love for God is love for God's own sake. Bernard of Clairvaux wrote that our natural inclination is to love for our own sake. When we learn to love God, we still love him for our own sake. As we grow in friendship with God, we come to love him not just for ourselves alone, but also for God's sake. At last, we may reach a point where we love even ourselves for the sake of God. **James Houston**[1]

[1] *The Transforming Friendship* (Lion Publishing, 1991), pp. 195-96.

4
If God Were Only Human!

Job 7:7-21; 9:14—10:7

W hen the bottom falls out of life, we cry: "Where is God when I am hurting? Does he really understand? Can he *do* anything? Does God dwell in heaven unmoved by our cries?"

Sometimes the Bible presents the most important truths not in a frontal attack or a prophetic pronouncement, but in a pregnant hint. This study is a case in point. It takes us one step farther to the edge of the greatest of all discoveries, the gospel itself—that God should become a human being, making himself totally accessible to his own creature.

---

1. Try to remember your first pictures or impressions of God. Was God distant, close, awesomely different, totally unlike anyone human, or very similar to your earthly father or mother? Explain.

---

2. Job's friends talk *about* God; Job talks *to* God. Read Job 7:7-21. Job now turns from complaining about his friends to complaining about his God—*to* God. In a few words summarize the matters Job raises with God.

Which complaints can you personally identify with?

3. Job is concerned that God will eventually discover that Job cannot be found (v. 8) if God keeps up the pressure. What does this tell us about Job's view of God?

4. Psychologists sometimes affirm that letting deep feelings spill out is emotionally healthy. Is it spiritually healthy? Explain why or why not.

Do you think God gets angry when we speak to him so negatively? Explain.

5. Job believes in God, but he cannot believe God is *for* him. What would Job's suffering be like without a belief in God?

6. Read Job 9:14—10:7. Why does Job feel it is becoming pointless to complain to God (9:14-20)?

Why is it equally pointless to put on a happy face (9:27-31)?

7. What does Job feel is wrong about his God (9:32-35 and 10:1-7)?

8. What specific benefits would Job gain if God were human (9:32) after all?

9. In none of his petitions does Job ask for his sickness to be cured. Describe what it is he wants from God.

10. In what ways has Jesus Christ made Job's deepest dream a reality?

11. When tragedy strikes, what difference does it make to know that God has come in the flesh (Jn 1:14)?

☐ I don't know Who—or what—put the question, I don't know when it was put. I don't even remember answering. But at some moment I did answer *Yes* to Someone—or something—and from that hour I was certain that existence is meaningful and that, therefore, my life, in self-surrender, had a goal. From that moment I have known what it means "not to look back," and "to take no thought for the morrow." **Dag Hammarskjold**[1]

---

[1]Quoted in Robert A. Raines, *Creative Brooding* (Macmillan (US), 1966), p. 112.

5
The Faith That Rebels
Job 13:1—14:17

Loss of work, loss of loved ones, loss of opportunities, excruciating disease and withering judgements from close friends—these are experiences against which people of faith can claim no immunity. But how should we respond? Simply accept them, fight them or try to ignore them?

No. Those who get blessed by God are not those who ask nothing of God but those who will do almost anything to know God. The kingdom is not for the mildly interested but the desperate (Gen 32:26). Jesus said it is for the hungry, the thirsty, the poor (Mt 5:3-6) and the bold (Lk 11:8). Job is a case in point.

Job experienced the loss of everything, even the comfort of his best friends. Yet Job refuses to give in, to accept his friends' explanations, or to accept the absence of God as God's final answer. There is more reverence in Job's "irreverence" than in the friends' deference to the inscrutability of God. This study will show us that faith sometimes requires us to rebel—in the right direction!

---

1. In what life experiences have you been tempted to "lie down and take it" or give up compliantly?

2. The third of Job's friends, Zophar, has delivered his message. Job knows that the ear tastes words "as the tongue tastes food" (12:11). What message has Job tasted from his friends so far?

---

3. Read Job 13. Why are the friends 'worthless physicians' (v. 4)?

---

4. What do you learn from this regarding caring for deeply needy people (v. 5)?

---

5. How has the well-intentioned "ministry" of the friends driven Job to something more fruitful than mere self-defense?

---

6. Job now speaks directly to God in verses 20-28. What does Job request of God (vv. 20-22)?

---

7. Read Job 14:1-17. What makes Job feel hopeless (14:7-12), even though he claims to have hope in God (13:15)?

---

8. How does the glimmer of hope in 13:15 compare and contrast with our full Christian hope in the New Testament?

9. If you could speak directly with God, what unanswered questions would you ask?

What unfair experiences would you want God to explain?

10. In what ways did Job rebel in the right direction?

11. What impact has this study had on your own response to the hardest experiences of life?

□ Zophar's wisdom is a bloodless retreat into theory. It is very proper, theologically familiar and unobjectionable. But it is flat beer compared with Job's seismic certainty.

Job still stands where he stood at first (1:21; 2:10), submissive to the irresistible might of God, but strained in faith as he fights to win his way to new assurance of the goodness of God. He is neither docile nor patient. **Francis Andersen**[1]

[1]Andersen, *Job*, pp. 156, 159.

6
Our Heavenly Guarantor

16:1—17:3; 19:23-27

W e long to be sure—sure that we are accepted by God, sure that our sins are *really* forgiven—not to crop up again to haunt us like a long-suppressed secret—sure that we will be with God when we die and sure that God is *for* us. Mike Mason suggests that one of our deepest questions is whether God likes us. "Of course God loves us, he loves everybody, indiscriminately, even the people he is going to send to hell. . . . The real question is not whether God loves us, but whether he approves of us, whether we are pleasing to him."[1] That question is now uppermost in Job's mind. As always, struggling toward an answer by talking to God, Job makes another breathtaking discovery, one which can bring life to every other generation. In the end our question—like Job's—is not "Is the universe friendly?" Rather, "Is there a Friend in the universe?"

---

1. Of what do you feel most sure in your life at this point? Explain.

---

2. Read Job 16:1—17:3. In chapter 15 Eliphaz started the second round of speeches, trying once again to cut Job down to size. What words does Job use to emphasize that not only his friends but also God have become his enemy (16:7-14)?

---

3. In what sense could Job say his "prayer is pure" (16:17)?

---

4. What certainty is impressed on Job's soul as he prays through his tears?

---

5. Job looks to God for a pledge of security. How is it possible that Job could appeal for help from God when it is God who is apparently attacking him?

---

6. Read Job 19:23-27. Bildad has had his second turn (chapter 18) at accusing Job. What grand assurance does Job's faith now claim?

---

7. In what ways does this great breakthrough answer the deepest quest of his prayers?

---

8. While discovering hope, Job must still exercise faith. Why is it important that the guarantees of our future should still require personal faith?

9. There are several images of God's provision in this study: witness, advocate, intercessor, guarantor, redeemer-kinsman. Which one especially gives you hope?

10. What difference will this make to the uncertainties you face?

11. What insecurities would you like to bring to your heavenly guarantor?

☐ The infinity of time and space separates us from God. How are we to seek for him? How are we to go towards him? Even if we were to walk for hundreds of years, we should do no more than go round and round the world. Even in an aeroplane we could not do anything else. We are incapable of progressing vertically. We cannot take a step toward the heavens. God crosses the universe and comes to us. Over the infinity of space and time, the infinitely more infinite love of God comes to possess us. He comes at his own time. We have the power to consent to receive him or to refuse. If we remain deaf he comes back again and again like a beggar, but also, like a beggar, one day he stops coming. If we consent, God puts a little seed in us and he goes away again. From that moment God has no more to do; neither have we, except to wait. We only have not to regret the consent we gave him, the nuptial yes. **Simone Weil**[2]

[1]Andersen, *Job*, p. 36.
[2]*Waiting on God*, trans. Emma Craufurd (Collins, 1950), p. 91.

7
The Problem of Pain
Job 20:1-19; 21:1-16

Wars, disease, congenital deformities, earthquakes and the seismic disturbances in our daily lives—all of these leave us with questions about the goodness of God and his active control of the world. Job himself suffered economic, familial, physical and social disaster, so much so that he despaired of life and longed for death.

How could a good God cause all this (as Job firmly believed), or even allow this (as most moderns would say)? The classic way of putting the matter is this: If God is all-powerful, he is not good; if he is good, he is not all-powerful. Or "if he is God he is not good; if he is good, then he is not God."

Job will not get his answer in the chapters we are studying. Indeed, he does not get a satisfying theological answer even in the end when God finally speaks—he will get something even better! But his dialogue with his friend Zophar will push his thinking and praying a step closer to the belief that God's love is not confined to rewards and punishments.

---

1. What have you witnessed or experienced in life that has made it difficult for you to believe there is a good God running the world?

2. Read Job 20:1-19. What words and phrases are used to describe the wicked in these verses?

3. Describe the punishment of the wicked.

4. What is Zophar's view of God's righteousness?

5. What is commendable about Zophar's theology?

What is problematic?

6. Read Job 21:1-16. How does Job's reality check contrast with Zophar's view (20:29)?

7. Job 21:14-15 expresses the spiritual question the wicked might ask: "What would we gain by praying to [God]?" On the basis of the discussion thus far, how do you think Zophar would answer that question?

How would Job reply?

---

8. It has been said that Job and the others were trying to fit together the pieces of a puzzle without having all the pieces. How can the discoveries Job is making (consider the last study too) help Job and us deal with the problem of pain?

---

9. How might Zophar have responded to the words of Jesus: our Father in heaven "causes his sun to shine on the evil and the good, and sends rain on the righteous and the unrighteous" (Mt 5:45)?

How might Job respond?

---

10. What have you learned in this study about helping people find answers to questions about the goodness of God?

How have your personal questions been addressed?

☐ We are as incapable as Job himself of fathoming the mystery of what God allows, and why. **Derek Kidner**[1]

---

[1] *The Wisdom of Proverbs, Job & Ecclesiastes* (InterVarsity Press (US), 1985), p 59.

8
The Silence of God
Job 23

The basic anatomy of the human being is profoundly suggestive: two ears and one mouth. Perhaps we should do twice as much listening as we do speaking. Certainly the friends of Job would have done much better had they listened twice as hard to Job's heart. "If only you would be altogether silent! For you, that would be wisdom" (13:5), said the word-weary Job.

We have all experienced someone's mindless chatter or withering judgment at a moment when we needed to be deeply understood. But when we listen—really listen—we "speak" with our ears. We communicate our respect, prize the person and encourage the movement of God in someone's life.

Could it be that it's the same with God? Does he communicate his love to us sometimes by listening as we pour out our hearts, rather than finishing our sentences for us and telling us how to feel, what to do, where to go?

For twenty-two chapters God has not spoken directly to Job. But God has listened in silence. And Job has spoken directly to God, indeed more and more directly. This study will explore the connection between Job's experience and our experience of the silence of God.

---

1. Recall a time when a friend or family member really listened to you. How did you feel?

How did that person's listening help you?

2. Read Job 23:1-12. What does Job now want more than anything (see also 29:4-5)?

Why does he want this?

3. Compare Job's fear of speaking with God in 9:14-20 with his new confidence in 23:6-7. How do you account for the change?

4. Why do you think Job finds God so elusive (vv. 8-9)?

5. Why do you think people sometimes find God unresponsive when they say they are seeking him wholeheartedly?

6. While Job does not know God (in the personal experiential sense, 42:5), he knows that God knows him (23:10-12). Why is this so comforting (see also Ps 139:1-18)?

7. Job longs for an opportunity to renew friendship with God and present his case, and he is not simply waiting passively. What has he been doing (vv. 10-12)?

8. How does Job's experience show the difference between a God who comforts through silence and an absent god who is not really there at all?

9. Job thinks of his suffering as a testing not to improve his character (as gold is refined by the fire) but to reveal his righteousness (as gold is proven to be what it truly is—gold). What gives Job confidence that he will "pass the test"?

10. Read Job 23:13-17. What appears to be Job's main remaining problem in establishing his righteousness with God?

11. In spite of Job's frustration in getting through to God, Job has not been silenced (v. 17). Why do you think this is so?

12. The Bible suggests that the people who received mystical experiences of God (Moses, Isaiah, John, and even Job—42:5) were not seeking an overwhelming encounter with God; these experiences were given by God at God's initiative. What does Job's case teach us about waiting?

How does Job's attitude help you to wait for God?

☐ My father himself never talked to me, except when we studied together. He taught me with silence. He taught me to look into myself, to find my own strength, to walk around inside myself in company with my soul. When his people would ask him why he was so silent with his son, he would say to them that he would not like to talk, words are cruel, words play tricks, they distort what is in the heart, they conceal the heart, the heart speaks through silence. One learns of the pain of others by suffering one's own pain, he would say, by turning inside oneself, by finding one's own soul. . . . For years his silence bewildered and frightened me, though I always trusted him, I never hated him. And when I was old enough to understand, he told me that of all people a tzaddik [saint] especially must know of pain. **Chaim Potok**[1]

---

[1] *The Chosen* (Fawcett Publications (US), 1967), p 265.

9
Songs in the Night
Job 35; 36:13-16

Kierkegaard once said that whatever it may be that one comes to as a matter of course because of ageing, it is not wisdom. So we see that Job's three friends, all senior, have tried to explain Job's suffering and to defend God. A tall order indeed, and not necessarily a good thing.

Now a young man, Elihu, comes into the picture. Elihu waited in the sidelines because, as he says, "Age should speak" (32:7). He is exasperated with Eliphaz, Bildad and Zophar because they have failed to deal adequately with Job. But he is also angry with Job "for justifying himself rather than God" (32:2). So he jumps into the discussion, offering his only slightly revised version of the stock answers, with one important variation. "If we needed any further warning against jumping to conclusions about particular cases, Elihu has certainly provided it."[1]

---

1. Recall a situation in your life when someone "jumped to a conclusion." How did you feel?

---

2. Read Job 35. In verse 3 Elihu claims that Job wants to know "What profit is it to me, and what do I gain by not sinning?" Yet Job has never said this. Why is this question important to the discussion?

3. How does Elihu answer the question he poses (vv. 4-8)?

4. What is Elihu's view of God?

5. Why is Elihu's answer to Job's (presumed) question not likely to satisfy Job, or anyone else in Job's situation?

6. In verses 9-16 Elihu deals with a second question—one that *was* asked by Job: Why doesn't God answer prayer? What is Elihu's answer to this question?

7. What truth is there in Elihu's answer?

What error?

8. Why does Elihu's "ministry" not offer any substantial help to Job?

9. Read Job 36:13-16. Elihu is trying to speak on God's behalf (36:2). How does he claim God ministers to people in their suffering?

10. Not all of Elihu's advice is misguided. He does propose that God, if he were sought, would give cheer and comfort in the night when things seem more hopeless than ever (35:10). When, if ever, have you received from God a "song in the night"?

11. This study concludes all the attempts of human beings to explain Job's situation and to comfort him. What have you learned about ministering to people in distress?

☐ My burden carries me. **Adolf Alexander Schroeders**[2]

[1]Kidner, *The Wisdom,* p. 70.
[2]*Die last tragt mich,* as quoted in Helmut Thielicke, *Und Wenn Gott Ware* (Qwee Verlag, Stuttgart: 1970), p. 238.

10
God in the Storm

Job 38:1-11, 31-41; 40:1-5

Surprise is one thing you can count on when dealing with the living God. We have had thirty-seven chapters of gut-wrenching dialogue between Job and his friends, heart-rending prayers by Job to his elusive God, and life-and-death questions hurled by Job at God to make sense of the suffering of the innocent. Job, we think, deserves a comprehensive answer from the supreme Being of the universe. He gets a surprise. For four chapters God speaks in the whirlwind. This is no "still small voice" speaking. God is thundering. But what he thunders is *more questions.*

Job wanted acquittal. God called him to worship. Strangest of all—Job seems to be more than satisfied with God's response! Perhaps Job was more satisfied than we are—which is a subject we will explore in this study.

---

1. What experiences of God have led you to worship?

---

2. Read Job 38:1-11, 31-41. What common theme do all of God's questions have?

3. Why does God emphasize that Job was not around when he created the world?

4. Why is it important for God to remind Job about what Job *cannot* do rather than what he can do?

5. What purpose can God have in telling Job that God does things which no human being will ever appreciate or even see?

6. What effect will all these questions have on Job's view of himself?

his view of God?

7. Read Job 40:1-5. What three words does God use to describe what Job has been doing up until now (40:2)?

8. Describe Job's first response to God's self-revelation (vv. 3-5).

9. Do you think that in every complaint against God there is an implicit revolt against our being creatures? Explain.

10. In what ways do God's questions address Job's deepest questions about God in the previous chapters?

11. Why do you think it is sometimes more important in our spiritual journey to get more questions than answers?

How have questions helped you to grow spiritually?

☐ The work of theology in our day is not so much interpretation as contemplation. . . . God and the world need to be held up for oohs and ahhs before they can be safely analyzed. Theology begins with admiration, not problems. **Robert Farrar Capon**[1]

[1] *An Offering of Uncles: The Priesthood of Adam and the Shape of the World* (Crossroad (US), 1982), p 163.

11
The Joy of Repentance

Job 40:6-14; 42:1-6

Hardly anyone would speak of repentance as desirable. But it is! Repentance is not joyless self-hatred but blessed God-discovery. Repentance is the experience of coming home.

We are now at the climax of the book. Job finally repents. *But of what?* That surely is one of the burning questions evoked by the book, the answer to which will provide a profound clue for our own spiritual journeys. Job is an exemplary saint (1:8) and has thus far rightly resisted caving in to his friends' insistence that he repent of a long list of moral failures. But Job is not exempt from the need to repent, as we will discover in this study.

---

1. How do you feel when someone tells you, "You *must* repent"?

---

2. Read Job 40:6-14. What indication is there that Job has not fully repented even though he is in a more subdued frame of mind?

3. What does God say Job has been doing in his attempt to justify himself (v. 8)?

How has Job done this?

---

4. Must self-justification necessarily be a slight on God's justice?

---

5. Through what means does God expand Job's grasp of his personal dilemma?

---

6. God now directs Job to consider two more awesome and untameable creatures (40:15—41:34). Job is moved to full repentance. Read Job 42:1-6. What words does Job use to describe his direct experience of God?

---

7. What does Job now know about God?

about himself?

about the moral structure of the universe?

8. Job's friends said, in effect, you *must* repent. God takes a different approach. Job was given no direct answer to his questions. On what is his repentance based?

9. What do you think it means for a person to "repent in dust and ashes"?

10. In what way can "despising oneself" be entirely healthy and holy?

In what way could it be unholy self-hatred?

11. What have you learned in this study about true repentance?

☐ As I see it, we shall never succeed in knowing ourselves unless we seek to know God. **St. Teresa**[1]

---

[1]As quoted in Elizabeth O'Connor, *Journey Inward, Journey Outward* (Harper & Row (US), 1968), p 17.

12
Is Faith Always Worthwhile?

Job 42:7-17

So what do we get out of it? money? power? success? There are some who would promise that faith will bring prosperity. But life doesn't usually meet those promises. Is it possible to love God without expectation of reward, or "for nothing"?

Every believer comes to these questions at some time or other. It is, after all, Satan's question in the first chapter. And so the fateful test is designed—the test to see whether Job's faith is without any ulterior motive or, as Satan believes, merely a commercial contract rather than a covenant of belonging.

After Job prays for his friends, he has his fortune restored and is given a new family. The story ends with Job living happily ever after and dying "old and full of years." But was Satan right? Is unselfish faith possible? or even desirable?

---

1. How do you react when you hear someone talking about the benefits of following Jesus (such as health and wealth) when you have never received some of these blessings?

---

2. Read Job 42:7-17. What do we now learn about God's evaluation of all the characters in the drama?

3. Job's friends would probably have agreed with all that God said to Job in chapters 38—41. Why is God angry with them?

4. In what sense has Job spoken of what is right about God (42:7)?

5. Note the reversed roles. What does Job now do for his friends which they should have done for him?

6. While Job's case is an individual one (a test case for Satan), what general application does verse 10 have for all followers of Jesus?

7. What possible significance can there be in the timing and context of Job's restored prosperity (v. 10)?

8. Some people regard the "happily ever after" ending of the story as an anticlimax, unsuitable to the spiritual breakthrough of 42:1-6. What does God's final blessing reveal about Job?

about God?

9. In what sense may suffering Christians look forward to the blessing of God?

10. How do you think Job would now answer the question "Why are you suffering?"

How could this answer be of help in caring for someone going through a season of affliction?

11. What is the answer to Satan's question "Does Job serve God for nothing?"

12. How is this question important to you?

13. What have you learned through this study about loving God for God's sake?

□ Mornington: "Would you say any kind of curiosity was wrong? What about Job?"

"Job?" the Archdeacon asked.

Mornington: "Well, Sir, I always understood that where Job scored over the three friends was in feeling a natural curiosity why all those unfortunate things happened to him. They simply put up with it, but he, so to speak, asked God what He thought He was doing."

The Vicar shook his head. "He was told he couldn't understand."

Mornington: "He was taunted with not being able to understand—which isn't quite the same thing. As a mere argument there's something lacking perhaps in saying to a man who's lost his money and his house and his family and is sitting on the dustbin, all over boils, 'Look at the hippopotamus.' "

"Job seemed to be impressed," the Archdeacon said mildly.

Mornington: "Yes, he was certainly a perfect fool, in one meaning or other of the words." **Charles Williams**[1]

---

[1] *War in Heaven*, as quoted in Samuel Terrien, *Job: Poet of Existence* (Bobbs-Merrill (US), 1957), p. 238.

Leader's Notes

Leading a Bible discussion can be an enjoyable and rewarding experience. But it can also be *scary*—especially if you've never done it before. If this is your feeling, you're in good company. When God asked Moses to lead the Israelites out of Egypt, he replied, "O Lord, please send someone else to do it!" (Ex 4:13).

When Solomon became king of Israel, he felt the task was beyond his abilities. "I am only a little child and do not know how to carry out my duties. . . . Who is able to govern this great people of yours?" (1 Kings 3:7, 9).

When God called Jeremiah to be a prophet, he replied, "Ah, Sovereign LORD, . . . I do not know how to speak; I am only a child" (Jer 1:6).

The list goes on. The apostles were "unschooled, ordinary men" (Acts 4:13). Timothy was young, frail and frightened. Paul's "thorn in the flesh" made him feel weak. But God's response to all of his servants—including you—is essentially the same: "My grace is sufficient for you" (2 Cor 12:9). Relax. God helped these people in spite of their weaknesses, and he can help you in spite of your feelings of inadequacy.

There is another reason why you should feel encouraged. Leading a Bible discussion is not difficult if you follow certain guidelines. You don't need to be an expert on the Bible or a trained teacher. The suggestions listed below should enable you to effectively and enjoyably fulfill your role as leader.

Preparing to Lead

1. Ask God to help you understand and apply the passage to your own life. Unless this happens, you will not be prepared to lead others. Pray too for the various members of the group. Ask God to give you an enjoyable and profitable time together studying his Word.

2. As you begin each study, read and reread the assigned Bible passage to familiarize yourself with what the author is saying. In the case of book studies, you may want to read through the entire book prior to the first study. This will give you a helpful overview of its contents.

3. This study guide is based on the New International Version of the Bible. It will help you and the group if you use this translation as the basis for your study and discussion. Encourage others to use the NIV also, but allow them the freedom to use whatever translation they prefer.

4. Carefully work through each question in the study. Spend time in meditation and reflection as you formulate your answers.

5. Write your answers in the space provided in the study guide. This will help you to express your understanding of the passage clearly.

6. It might help you to have a Bible dictionary handy. Use it to look up any unfamiliar words, names or places. (For additional help on how to study a passage, see chapter five of *Leading Bible Study Discussions* SU).

7. Once you have finished your own study of the passage, familiarize yourself with the leader's notes for the study you are leading. These are designed to help you in several ways. First, they tell you the purpose the study guide author had in mind while writing the study. Take time to think through how the study questions work together to accomplish that purpose. Second, the notes provide you with additional background information or comments on some of the questions. This information can be useful if people have difficulty understanding or answering a question. Third, the leader's notes can alert you to potential problems you may encounter during the study.

8. If you wish to remind yourself of anything mentioned in the leader's notes, make a note to yourself below that question in the study.

Leading the Study

1. Begin the study on time. Unless you are leading an evangelistic Bible study, open with prayer, asking God to help you to understand and apply the passage.

2. Be sure that everyone in your group has a study guide. Encourage them to prepare beforehand for each discussion by working through the questions in the guide.

3. At the beginning of your first time together, explain that these studies are meant to be discussions not lectures. Encourage the members of the group to participate. However, do not put pressure on those who may be hesitant to speak during the first few sessions.

4. Read the introductory paragraph at the beginning of the discussion. This will orient the group to the passage being studied.

5. Read the passage aloud if you are studying one chapter or less. You may choose to do this yourself, or someone else may read if he or she has been asked to do so prior to the study. Longer passages may occasionally be read in parts at different times during the study. Some studies may cover several chapters. In such cases reading aloud would probably take too much time, so the group members should simply read the assigned passages prior to the study.

6. As you begin to ask the questions in the guide, keep several things in mind. First, the questions are designed to be used just as they are written. If you wish, you may simply read them aloud to the group. Or you may prefer to express them in your own words. However, unnecessary rewording of the questions is not recommended.

Second, the questions are intended to guide the group toward understanding and applying the *main idea* of the passage. The author of the guide has stated his or her view of this central idea in the *purpose* of the study in the leader's notes. You should try to understand how the passage expresses this idea and how the study questions work together to lead the group in that direction.

There may be times when it is appropriate to deviate from the study guide. For example, a question may have already been answered. If so, move on to the next question. Or someone may raise an important question not covered in the guide. Take time to discuss it! The important thing is to use discretion. There may be many routes you can travel to reach the goal of the study. But the easiest route is usually the one the author has suggested.

7. Avoid answering your own questions. If necessary, repeat or rephrase them until they are clearly understood. An eager group quickly becomes passive and silent if they think the leader will do most of the talking.

8. Don't be afraid of silence. People may need time to think about the question before formulating their answers.

9. Don't be content with just one answer. Ask, "What do the rest of you think?" or "Anything else?" until several people have given answers to the question.

10. Acknowledge all contributions. Try to be affirming whenever possible. Never reject an answer. If it is clearly wrong, ask, "Which verse led you to that conclusion?" or again, "What do the rest of you think?"

11. Don't expect every answer to be addressed to you, even though this will probably happen at first. As group members become more at ease, they will begin to truly interact with each other. This is one sign of a healthy discussion.

12. Don't be afraid of controversy. It can be very stimulating. If you don't resolve an issue completely, don't be frustrated. Move on and keep it in mind for later. A subsequent study may solve the problem.

13. Stick to the passage under consideration. It should be the source for answering the questions. Discourage the group from unnecessary cross-referencing. Likewise, stick to the subject and avoid going off on tangents.

14. Periodically summarize what the *group* has said about the passage. This helps to draw together the various ideas mentioned and gives continuity to the study. But don't preach.

15. Conclude your time together with conversational prayer. Be sure to ask God's help to apply those things which you learned in the study.

16. End on time.

Many more suggestions and helps are found in *Leading Bible Study Discussions* (SU). Reading and studying through that would be well worth your time.

Components of Small Groups

A healthy small group should do more than study the Bible. There are four components you should consider as you structure your time together.

Nurture. Being a part of a small group should be a nurturing and edifying experience. You should grow in your knowledge and love of God and each other. If we are to properly love God, we must know and keep his commandments (Jn 14:15). That is why Bible study should be a foundational part of your small group.

But you can be nurtured by other things as well. You can memorize Scripture, read and discuss a book, or occasionally listen to a tape of a good speaker.

Community. Most people have a need for close friendships. Your small group can be an excellent place to cultivate such relationships. Allow time for informal interaction before and after the study. Have a time of sharing during the meeting. Do fun things together as a group, such as a potluck supper or a picnic. Have someone bring refreshments to the meeting. Be creative!

Worship. A portion of your time together can be spent in worship and prayer. Praise God together for who he is. Thank him for what he has done and is doing in your lives and in the world. Pray for each other's needs. Ask God to help you to apply what you have learned. Sing hymns together.

Mission. Many small groups decide to work together in some form of outreach. This can be a practical way of applying what you have learned. You can host a series of evangelistic discussions for your friends or neighbors. You can visit people at a home for the elderly. Help a widow with cleaning or repair jobs around her home. Such projects can have a transforming influence on your group.

For a detailed discussion of the nature and function of small groups, read *Small Group Starter Kit* or *Growing Christians in Small Groups* (both from SU).

Study 1. Dueling with the Devil. Job 1:1—2:10.

Purpose: To probe good and bad reasons for spiritual life.

General Note: In the Hebrew text *Satan* is not a proper name but a simple description of his action: the accuser. However, for the purposes of this study the name *Satan* will be used.

Question 1. Every study begins with an "approach" question, which is meant to be asked before the passage is read. These questions are important for several reasons.

First, they help the group to warm up to each other. No matter how well a group may know each other, there is always a stiffness that needs to be overcome before people will begin to talk openly. A good question will break the ice.

Second, approach questions get people thinking along the lines of the topic of the study. Most people will have lots of different things going on in their minds (dinner, an important meeting coming up, how to get the car fixed) that will have nothing to do with the study. A creative question will get their attention and draw them into the discussion.

Third, approach questions can reveal where our thoughts or feelings need to be transformed by Scripture. That is why it is especially important not to read the passage before the approach question is asked. The passage will tend to color the honest reactions people would otherwise give because they are, of course, supposed to think the way the Bible does. Giving honest responses before they find out what the Bible says may help them see where their thoughts or attitudes need to be changed:

This approach question begins a process of reflection that will integrate all twelve studies. Two conflicting charges are often leveled against believers: first their faith is just a crutch to support them through life's rough spots, and second, their faith is a fair-weather religion which is untested. When the benefits of believing are no longer apparent, believers will abandon their devotion.

Though the second charge was Satan's approach, both accusations have a common thread: religion is a contract between the believer and God. The believer supplies devotion; God provides benefits. Such a commercial (rather than covenantal) approach to faith is deeply rooted in human experience. But true biblical faith is fundamentally the worship and enjoyment of God because he is God.

As we shall see, Job does not know about Satan's charge, and he attributes *to the wicked* such thoughts as "What would we gain by praying to [God]?" (21:15). Job's friend Eliphaz, taking up a similar thread, adds that if faith seems resultless to humankind, it is also resultless to God: "What pleasure would it give the Almighty if you were righteous?" (22:3). Both are probing the question behind the questions, "Why trust God?" This question will be answered in this book not by a rational argument but by truth strained through the experience of one exceptional human being.

Question 2. While almost everyone can identify with Job because his experience is so universal, Job himself is not everyman. He is a real, though very exceptional human being of whom even God is rightly proud (1:8; 2:3). He can be listed with Noah and Daniel (Ezek 14:14).

Job came from the Land of the East (1:3) which is a general description of the area east of the Jordan. While we do not know that he was an Israelite, he certainly worshiped Israel's God and gained a spirituality that harmonized prayer ("feared God") and ethics ("shunned evil"), both positive and negative, matters to which Job himself (chapters 29—31), Job's friends (4:3-6) and God himself (42:8) attest.

The reference to "the morning after the party" sacrifice on behalf of his children shows Job acting as priest of his family, interceding lest any of them commit the sin Satan wants him to commit—cursing God (1:11; 2:5).

In his masterful commentary Francis Andersen takes up the relation of Job's righteousness with the doctrine of universal human depravity. Andersen shows that even Job is convinced he is sinful but "it is possible for sinful men to be genuinely good. It may be rare, but it is possible for a man who loves and obeys God" (*Job: An Introduction and Commentary*, Tyndale Old Testament Commentaries [InterVarsity Press, 1976], p. 79. And Job is such a person.

Question 3. It is all too easy to "read into" this story Satan pictured in the Gospels and the Red Dragon of the Revelation. Taken within the context of this book alone several remarkable features stand out about Satan: (1) His name may not be a proper name but descriptive of his activity *the* accuser or adversary. Satan appears as a proper name only once in the Old Testament (1 Chron 21:1). (2) He is part of the divine council, the heavenly host (1 Ki 22:19; Ps 103:20; Zech 1:10ff.; Ps 89:7) who attend God but are not his colleagues. Satan is one of the sons of God. (3) Just as there is no polytheism here, there is no dualism—"The Satan may be the chief mischief-maker of the universe, but he is a mere creature, puny compared with the Lord" (Andersen, *Job*, p. 83). (4) Satan has a minor role in the book, not appearing again after 2:7. Andersen says, "It is impossible to believe that the purpose of this tremendous book is to teach us an explanation of evil that Job and his friends never think of, namely that human suffering is caused by the Devil" (*Job*, p. 83).

Professor N. H. Snaith summarizes Satan's role as "God's Inspector-of-man on earth and man's adversary in heaven" (quoted in E. S. P. Heavenor, "Job," *The New Bible Commentary*, ed. F. Davidson, A. M. Stibbs and E. F. Kevan, 2nd ed. [Inter-Varsity Fellowship, 1954], pp. 388-89).

Questions 4-5. The nature of the struggle is complex indeed. The action of Satan takes place in the presence of God, but we are not told where. The real contest is not between Satan and Job (spiritual warfare of a human being with the devil) but between God and Satan.

Mike Mason says, "It is a celestial battle, fought on earth, a sort of duel between good and evil" so that "human beings, soul and body, are the duelling ground where the heavenly powers clash" ("The Wizard of Uz: Meditations on Job" *Crux* 27, [June 1991]:37). He suggests that a duel is a better metaphor for the conflict than spiritual warfare since God could have blasted his puny Satan, but in a duel, equivalent weapons are chosen and the contest is kept *fair*. God's omnipotence is never in question. "But what is being disputed in dubious battles on earth is God's moral *right* to omnipotence, his mandate to rule" (Mason, "Wizard," p. 38).

So there is a contest which is not exactly a wager because there are no stakes. In this contest it turns out that God knows his Job better than Satan does—which is no small comfort to the rest of us. Untested faith is immature faith (Jas 1:2-8), and we have a God who takes risks with those he loves. Some sicknesses or disasters may be God's permissive will allowed for some greater good now hidden from our eyes, as it was (initially) hidden from Job.

Not only is the purpose of the duel kept from Job, but so is God's unqualified admiration of Job, until the end (42:7), though it will be clear from Job's agonizing prayers that follow that both he and we long for God's approval more than anything.

The basic questions of the book are now before us: "Is God so good he can be loved for Himself, not just for his gifts? Can a man hold on to God when there are no benefits attached?" (Andersen, *Job*, p. 85).

Question 6. For Job—as well as many believers—faith does not reduce the suffering but rather causes it. Job responds in faith not only by showing the culturally appropriate outer signs of grief and bereavement, but by worshiping God inwardly by seeing God's hand in it all, though he knows not why. Job honors God and his blessings even when circumstances appear to shout the denial of the goodness of God.

Question 7. The secularist, the fatalist, the atheist and the hedonist do not have Job's problem, but neither will they have his ultimate blessing (42:5). Others will talk about their rights and so charge God with wrongdoing, but Job believes God to be absolutely sovereign. Those pressing their rights reject creatureliness (and their Creator) and thus find life to be ultimately tragic. In contrast, by accepting creatureliness and the Sovereign Lord, Job can live in hope even while contemplating his own death.

Question 9. See the notes on questions 4-5 for the issues surrounding the first test. Though the Lord says in 2:3 that he has ruined Job "without any reason," there *was* a reason in the first test: to prove Satan wrong and to prove Job right. But the Hebrew word here also means "futile" or "in vain," which may be closer to the true meaning: Satan has got nowhere with God or Job.

Satan's first round in the contest has failed, so now he proposes the loss of Job's health. Later references highlight some of the symptoms of Job's unnamed disease: emaciation (19:20), fever (30:30), depression (7:16; 30:15), weeping (16:16), sleeplessness (7:4), nightmares (7:14), bad breath (19:17), failing vision (16:16) and rotting teeth (19:20). Sitting on the ash heap—now an obvious outcast from the community—Job, according to the Greek translation of the book, used a potsherd to scrape the pus off his sores.

God is still in charge, however, and Job's life must be spared (2:6). Even in this God would not allow his beloved creature to be tempted above what he is able to stand (1 Cor 10:13). Job, as we will soon see, longed for death as a way of escape, but God provided another way.

Derek Kidner comments helpfully of the morality of the contest and suggests that this concession to Satan was not merely an isolated tactic but a consistent practice. "God's chosen way was not to crush (evil) out of hand but to wrestle with it; and to do so in weakness rather than in strength, through men more often than through miracles, and through costly permissions rather than through flat refusals . . . overcoming it in fair combat, not by veto but by hard-won victory" (*The Wisdom of Proverbs, Job & Ecclesiastes* [InterVarsity Press (US), 1985], p. 59).

Question 10. Literally becoming Satan's advocate, Job's wife proposed that her husband do exactly what Satan had predicted. Apparently, in questioning whether Job's faith has done any good for him, she had already lost her faith and wanted her husband to join her as Eve does with Adam (Gen 3:1-6). Though in the first temptation the issue was the presumed *benefits* of rejecting single-minded obedience (Gen 3:5), in this case the issue was the apparent *nonbenefit* of believing. In both Genesis and Job the issue is that faith must not be not founded on personal gain or disqualified by personal loss.

In spite of his wife's provocation, and later his friends', Job *refused* to sin by cursing God through insisting on his own rights. As Andersen shows (*Job*, p. 93), Job responds to the first contest by insisting it is equally right for God to give gifts and to retrieve them, and to the second contest by insisting it is equally right for God to send good or bad and to do so without attributing wickedness in God. Adding to Job's suffering is the breakdown of all intimate relationships including, as we will see, that with his friends.

Question 11. A remarkable commentary on Job by a South American theologian suggests that the West has not had a theology of the evil of misfortune, the evil suffered by the innocent, no-fault suffering. Gustavo Gutiérrez, speaking of the final "answer" given to Job about his suffering by the Lord in the whirlwind speech, says, "The truth [Job] has grasped and that has lifted him to the level of contemplation is that justice alone does not have the final say about how we are to speak of God. Only when we have come to realize that God's love is freely bestowed do we enter fully and definitively into the God of faith" (*On Job: God-Talk and the Suffering of the Innocent*, trans. Matthew J. O'Connell [Orbis (US), 1987], p. 87). God's love—and true faith—does not operate in a world of cause and effects, but in freedom and grace.

Study 2. God in the Dark. Job 2:11—4:17.

Purpose: To find responses to suffering that are helpful and honoring to God.

Question 4. In cursing the day of his birth Job is not cursing the God who so marvelously created him. In 10:8 Job attributes to God both the physical shaping of his life, with a possible allusion to sperm in 10:10, and the moral formation of his personhood (10:12). Yet he also says that he loathes his life (10:1), wishes he were never born, had died at birth (3:11), or could die now (3:11-19). He curses neither God nor himself. Later Job will question God, but for the moment he moans (3:24-26) about his own miserable and apparently cursed existence. God may be responsible but God's goodness is not in question—not yet!

Question 5. As Job pounds out his complaint, he does so *both*—as will be apparent even more in later speeches—to God and to his friends. The speeches from chapters 3—31 have a unique character. They are not merely dramatic speeches in a play. This is not merely an intellectual exercise or a debate. It is hard even to characterize the "positions" of Job's three friends. And the conversation of Job and his friends is not truly a dialogue. Job's friends are trying to make their points, usually in line with conventional religious maxims such as "God gives people what they deserve," while Job, rejecting the conventional wisdom, tries to make sense of his life by talking to himself, to his friends, and supremely to his God, making him "the only authentic theologian in the book" (Andersen, *Job,* p. 98).

Questions 6-7. While Job considers what it would be like if he did not exist, or never had, he also takes up the case for all of humanity—for those who seem to be born for trouble. One thinks of the poorest of the poor, those born and raised in concentration camps and refugee villages, who grow up to be a despised minority, who never receive advantages, whose life appears to be senseless and meaningless, who just survive. Is Job's suffering greater because he has known prosperity, known joy, known the presence of God? In this book suicide is never contemplated because, presumably, death as well as life must be God's gift. What bothers Job is not only the physical suffering but the spiritual darkness, experiencing the absence of God (see 29:2-3) and feeling hedged in by God (3:23). God is absent in the way he has known in the past (as friend) and present as enemy! Job's passionate outburst against God's negative involvement in his life hints that the godly way may not always be to make reason triumph over passion, or to have "a stiff upper lip." Job is in line with the Psalms, Jeremiah 20:14-18, Lamentations 3:1-18 and the agony of Jesus (Mt 27:46). He "tells it all" to God in the presence of his friends. This is not only emotionally healthy but a key to Job's perseverance (Jas 5:11).

Question 8. Eliphaz tries to encourage Job, but he does so by insisting Job "practice what he has preached," so rendering his present discouragement morally wrong. He accuses Job of not *feeling* differently. Instead of letting Job have his own experience, Eliphaz and the others try to encourage by giving reasonable answers to Job's questions. Eliphaz's logic is straightforward: sinners suffer consequences (4:7-11); Job is suffering; therefore Job is a sinner. Eliphaz calls Job to appeal to God (5:8—the very thing he will do) and to accept the "blessing" of the Lord's correction and discipline (5:17) because God not only wounds but heals (5:18). Cold comfort indeed.

In contrast God (in this book) encourages by his silence, and ultimately by giving Job the big view—expanding his vision to have a God-sized view of reality. Ironically, God's non-answer to Job's discouragement incited Job to prayer; the friends' verbal approach incited Job to self-justification. Again, ironically, the friends' accusations forced Job to stumble on some good news—Job is accepted by God not because of his impeccable record but because of his faith—justification by faith alone.

Questions 9-10. Eliphaz operates on a widely held universal principle that moral effort is worthwhile, and immorality results in suffering (4:8). He and his friend conclude from this that Job must be suffering because he is a sinner. Job, therefore, must conclude that, because he is convinced of his innocence, God is unjust. Eliphaz's appeal to Job's faith involves admitting his sin and turning to God; Job's faith leads him to question God. Eliphaz maintains that God's ways are beyond ours, inscrutable (5:9). Eliphaz uses the mystery of God to prove he is right and Job is wrong—you can't understand it, so why don't you just accept it? Job later comes to the same conclusion but as a matter of faith. Eliphaz reveals that the real authority for his ministry to his friend is not in God but in his own theology. He has God under control even though he claims that God dwells in a mystery. It is another great irony that Job's piety *was* his confidence, but for reasons different from those proposed by Eliphaz and his friends.

Francis Andersen offers a helpful New Testament perspective on the matter under discussion—whether good and bad get what they deserve: "Paul makes clear what Job gropes after. This faith will be broken by life, unless it is held eschatologically, in hope; for the 'harvest is the close of the age' (Mt. 13:39), and Eliphaz's truth will be seen only 'on that day when . . . God judges the secrets of men by Christ Jesus' (Rom. 2:16)" (*Job*, p. 113).

Study 3. God-Talk: How Not to Be Spiritual Friends. Job 6.

Purpose: To understand some dimensions of spiritual friendship through concrete examples.

Question 1. The concept of "spiritual friend" may be a new one. Simply put, a spiritual friend is another person who walks with you on your spiritual journey, encouraging you in your life of faith, fanning the coals of your passion for God, listening to your heart, cultivating the life of prayer. Spiritual friendship is not counseling, not directing, not judging, not teaching. It is a side-by-side relationship of trust in which each can tell an unedited version of one's inner life, and do so in the presence of God for mutual upbuilding. Tragically, most followers of Christ today do not have such relationships, even in the church!

Question 2. Eliphaz starts with some discretion (4:2) but then seems to unload his pent-up frustration and anger. Instead of continuing to listen, Eliphaz attacks. He claims to point Job toward God ("I would appeal to God," 5:8) and exhorts him to hold on to God's promise of blessing and healing (5:17-19).

Job is grieved and hurt by his friends and eventually becomes irritated and angry.

His only hope in the end is in God, to whom he continuously turns, but more *in spite of* the spiritual help of his friends than because of it! In particular 5:9-27 shows that Eliphaz views God as awesome, holy, manifestly just in all his dealings with the evildoers (vv. 12-13), compassionate with the poor (vv. 15-16) and gracious to the person (like Job) who is being corrected by God (vv. 17-26). Eliphaz ends his speech from a presumed superior spiritual position (v. 27). His non-help is related to his view of God, his view of Job, his understanding of divine chastisement and his view of himself.

Reflecting on the book as a study in pastoral care, William Hulme says: "Eliphaz' purpose is to shame Job into silence. If we can make a person feel guilty, we can control him. This is the most effective kind of domination because it is domination from within the person. By manipulating his conscience we can tyrannize his spirit" (*Dialogue in Despair* [Abingdon (US), 1968], p. 28).

Question 3. Job feels that God is against him, even more. that ⌐ ¬ ⌐ picking him out for target practice (v. 4). If God is responsible for everything, then he must be the cause. Coming as many do from a society that is essentially secular, we may find this hard to grasp, though it is a challenging change of perspective. The alternative— that God is not directly responsible and is helpless before a fateful process outside his control—has greater problems.

Job's request that God would crush him to death is tied to the expected consolation that he had "not denied the words of the Holy One" (v. 10). Job is still righteous, but he does not know whether he can hold on. He would rather die now than lose his spiritual integrity. All of this is said as a prayer to God even though Job speaks about God in the third person—a conventional manner of speaking respectfully to a superior (Andersen, *Job*, p. 129). Job speaks *to* God (for example, directly in 7:7-21); his friends speak *about* God. His friends would have been better to talk to God about their friend rather than talking about God to Job.

Question 4. The metaphors pile up images of frustrated hope for help. The word pictures find their origin in the waters of Israel that can be dry one day, a roaring stream the next and then dry again—frustrating weary travelers counting on refreshment. Job himself eventually categorizes his friends as "miserable comforters" (16:2). But the book does not picture Job's friends as hypocrites or heretics. In fact some of Eliphaz's words are quoted in the New Testament as inspired Scripture (5:13 with 1 Cor 3:19; 5:17 with Heb 12:5). Derek Kidner comments that "the basic error of Job's friends is that they overestimate their grasp of truth, misapply the truth they know, and close their minds to any facts that contradict what they assume" (Kidner, *The Wisdom*, p. 61). What kept them from being soul friends was not false doctrine but theological arrogance.

Question 5. Verse 14 is notoriously difficult to translate, and commentators (see Andersen, *Job*, p. 130 and H. H. Rowley, *The Book of Job*, New Century Bible Commentary [Marshall, Morgan & Scott (HarperCollins Publishers), 1981], pp. 61-62) cannot agree whether it is Job or Eliphaz who is forsaking the fear of the Lord by failing to show covenant loyalty ("kindness")—Job by failing in his personal loyalty to God or Eliphaz in failing to show kindness to his friend. The RSV translates the verse "He who withholds kindness from a friend forsakes the fear of the Almighty". Either way, Job is registering the failure of his friend to show him kindness at his moment of need, a matter which Job claimed his own religion considered fundamental (29: 12-17).

Question 6. Like Eliphaz, we struggle to remain affectionately loyal (two dimensions implied in covenant love) with people close to us when they cannot embrace our view of God's ways, or they go through a dark night of the soul. It is all too easy to avoid relationship with a person who, we suspect, is under the displeasure of God. Sometimes we fear being polluted by association. Paul dealt in the New Testament with a different though related circumstance of a believing wife finding herself in a covenant with an unbelieving husband (1 Cor 7:12-14). Paul pointed to the positive influence which the believer can give, though, as Peter advises, an influence to be expressed in life rather than sermons (1 Pet 3:1-2).

Questions 7-8. The progression of the friends' attacks can be traced through the book. After finding Job intransigent on the issue of his suffering because of personal sin, the friends move from gently probing for secret sins to outright attack (chapter 15). In language reminiscent of the suffering servant, Job can cry, "Men open their mouths to jeer at me, they strike my cheek in scorn and unite together against me" (16:10, compare with Is 50:6; 53:3). The friends invent a list of terrible sins which they claim he must have committed (22:5-11) in their attempt to defend the justice and honor of God, an action often taken by zealous defenders of God but which is soundly denounced not only by Job (13:7-9) but by God (42:7).

The reasons for their misguided, unkind strategy are not only a failure in their own faith—a failure to welcome and to live with mystery—but their own insecurities. Sprinkled throughout the dialogues are Job's assessments of the real reasons for the attacks of the friends: his disaster awakened fear in them, perhaps that something dreadful could happen to them (6:21); they felt superior (12:5; 13:2); they felt their honor was threatened by Job's protestations (18:3) and rebukes (20:3). Eventually, Elihu will vindictively pray, "Oh, that Job might be tested to the utmost" (34:36).

One of the great challenges of spiritual friendship is to welcome our friends as they are, even when we have no explanation for their experience, and there is nothing we can *do* to change their situation. What we can do is create a space in our hearts where they can be free. Without such inspired hospitality we may try to control the person when we cannot explain their experience. Those wishing to explore the pastoral implications of the dialogues may consult William E. Hulme's *Dialogue in Despair.*

Question 9. Commenting on 12:5, Rowley says, "Job is observing that the theology of the friends is the theology of the prosperous, who can afford to look down on the unfortunate and excuse themselves from giving sympathy by the assumption that they have brought it upon themselves" (*The Book of Job,* p. 92). Job himself, once a prosperous man, did not allow his wealth to insulate him from the poor and powerless (29:12-17) and even now—perhaps because of this—in his extreme suffering and loss he takes up the cause of suffering humanity (24:1-25).

Though this is not the message of the book of Job, the Bible does suggest that the rich need the poor and that some form of voluntary impoverishment is crucial to the true godliness of the rich, a matter which Job apparently understood intuitively. The importance of this for soul friends cannot be overstated. Compassion shown in times of relative prosperity—whether material or spiritual—prepares us to give and receive compassion in times of poverty and need—whether material or spiritual.

Question 10. The NIV text note suggests that "integrity" (v. 29) could also be translated "righteousness." This brings us again to the heart of the matter. God is convinced Job is a righteous man (1:8). Satan admits Job is righteous, but questions whether it is *disinterested* righteousness. The friends, operating from their cause-effect theology, cannot believe Job could be righteous while suffering the obvious displeasure of God. Job is adamant: he knows he is not suffering because he is a sinner, and he knows he has integrity before God. Ironically, his friends' accusations and his own internal witness to being righteous will drive him not to mere self-justification but to a discovery of the gospel in the Old Testament.

Study 4. If God Were Only H~~~~~~~ ~~~~~ ~~~, 9:14—10:7.

~~D~~~~~ ~~~~~~~~ ~~~ ~~~ meaning of the Incarnation—that God should become a human being.

Question 1. For some people the humanity of God is precisely their problem—God is pictured as a projection of their earthly father or mother, often making belief emotionally intolerable and spiritually paralyzing. In the end we are not *convinced* about the fatherhood of God (by reflecting on our experience of being parented) but *converted* to it. Other people will, like Job, struggle with God's absolute transcendence, making God unapproachable and unknowable. Christians claim that the problem of imagining God is answered by the Incarnation (God's having revealed himself through a complete human life). God has made himself known, whispering baby talk to our ears, yet not in such an overwhelming way that the need for faith is eliminated.

Questions 2-3. Job's complaints make an impressive list: (1) his life is too short for God to make all this happen to him, (2) God will look for him and miss him when he finally dies, (3) he doesn't want to live this way forever and doesn't *want* eternal life if this is what it will be like, (4) he feels God is using him for target practice, and (5) when it is all over God will look for him and be disappointed that Job is no more.

Scholars are uncertain whether verses 17-19 are a parody on Psalm 8 or whether Job's "hymn" came first. Instead of rejoicing (as Psalm 8 does) in the amazing concern of God for his human creature, Job feels that God is the heavenly inspector. So Job wants some privacy (7:19), at least for a breather. Going deeper still, Job wants to know why God has not forgiven him *if* he is still in sin (v. 21). As Andersen says, "The reader knows that this stand of Job is entirely correct. His sufferings are so beyond the proportion of any sin he knows of that there must be some explanation beyond the categories of sin and punishment" (*Job*, p. 139).

Question 4. In contrast to Eliphaz, who believes that prayer is pointless because no one is listening (5:1), Job believes he is not a "mere" creature but a person lovingly and awesomely created by the living God (10:8-12). So he insists on the "right" of asking his questions directly to God even if the questions are unanswerable, as it turns out they largely are. But this questioning is not merely therapeutic. It is spiritually productive, because Job's highest desire is not merely for answers but for the "friendship of God" (29:4).

Pleading his case as boldly and artlessly as he does, Job reveals a heart determined to find meaning. The preacher in Ecclesiastes 1:1-2, in contrast, also judged life to be futile but got mired in sourness, in part because he did not pursue his questions, as Job did, to their final answer (Andersen, *Job*, p. 134). Perhaps bad prayers are better than no prayers.

God's final revelation to Job in chapters 38—41 does not contain a criticism of Job's prayer life, though God does accuse Job of condemning God in order to justify himself (40:8). God (astonishingly) says that Job has spoken well of his creator (42:7). What God criticizes and what Job must repent of is a subject of a later study.

Question 5. Job has not yet concluded that this negative attention from God is better than no "attention" at all, or experiencing deep suffering without any reference to God at all. Superficially, one might think it makes it "easier" to believe in the goodness of God if God is not *directly* responsible for everything bad that "happens." But then God would not be the author of good. In the end, as we shall see, the answer will lie beyond simple cause-effect. True faith in God will not be under human rational control. It is wholehearted abandon to God that is almost violent in nature because of its intensity (Mt 11:12). Job has such faith—as will soon be apparent—and God will approve of his faith.

Question 6. In chapter 9 Job stumbles on the folly of hoping in a God-man. But his reasons are largely negative. In the first section (9:2-13) he complains God is *arbitrary*—omnipotent in nature (9:5-10) and not controlled in anger (9:13). Then (9:14-24) Job claims God is *elusive*—whether God summons Job (9:14-15) or Job summons God (9:16-20), God will likely discriminate in favor of the wicked. Though he believes he is truly innocent he would, if given an audience, end up condemning himself in the presence of such an awesome judge (9:20). Finally (9:25—10:7), Job concludes that his plight is hopeless because God is *inhuman*. A just decision is impossible because Job is human and God is not. But if God were human, Job would have an accessible God and friendship with God—something for which Job longed even more than justice (23:3; 29:4).

Questions 7-8. Job's problem is complex. He is convinced simultaneously that he is innocent and that God holds him guilty (9:29). So Job explores his need for a mediator ("someone to arbitrate between us," 9:33), a phrase translated in the RSV as "umpire." Unlike his friends, who advise a religious remedy, Job knows that self-medication is pointless (9:30). He needs someone who can lay his hands on both Job and God as a common friend, a negotiator (see Is 1:18)—not a judge who would decide his case. Strahan observes "that while Job is ostensibly pleading for justice, deep down he is seeking for reconciliation, and finds here an unconscious prophecy of incarnation and atonement" (Rowley, *The Book of Job*, p. 82).

In all of this there are two redeeming features to Job's spiritual quest. First, he views God as essentially unmanageable. Bildad can apply cause-effect logic to the science of knowing God (8:4-5); Job knows he must learn to live with mystery and will never know more than the "outer fringe of his works" (26:14). Job fears God (1:8). Second, while the friends watch and talk, Job explores God's ways.

Questions 10-11. In an important passage in his commentary Francis Andersen notes:

> The gospel of Christ has not brought to any man a guarantee of less misery than Job's. It has brought rather the sharing of Christ's sufferings (Phil. 3:10), without which a person is but half a Christian. . . . And every distinguished forerunner of Christ in the Old Testament had to become 'a man of sorrows' (Is. 53:3)—Abraham, Jacob, Joseph, Moses, Ruth, Hannah, David, Hosea, Jeremiah—the list is long. Job is in this succession, and there is something he will find out about God as his Saviour which is much more than protection from harm or rescue from trouble. It is much more important for God to be with him in his trouble. This is what he is seeking in prayer. (*Job,* pp. 152-53)

Study 5. The Faith That Rebels. Job 13:1—14:17.

Purpose: To di~~scover~~ the place of godly rebellion in the life of faith.

Question 2. Derek Kidner notes that Job feels under attack from two quarters at once: from his God and his friends. Job is hurt that his friends concern themselves with what he has done (on the assumption that he is suffering as a sinner) rather than what *God* has done. In response Job has reproached (6:26) and accused (13:4, 7-8) them. Eventually, he will mock them (21:3), hold them in contempt (21:34). But he does hold a pastoral concern for them, as evidenced in 13:7-11, a pastoral concern that finds its consummation, ironically, in his eventual prayer for their restoration to God (42:8-9). He proves to be their friend in the end in spite of their failure to be his. While Job is discovering the self-interest of his so-called friends, Job's friendship with God is being tested and proven to be remarkably free from self-interest (23:10).

Question 3. Undoubtedly the friends attack Job (11:6) because his pain threatens them (6:21; 18:3). They too could be similarly afflicted and need some rational basis of assuring themselves "that it couldn't happen to them." But there is further, deeper reason. Their theology does not explain how the Job they knew could suffer—unless he was a sinner in some way they had not known before.

They will soon be in the sad situation of feeling a secret pleasure when they discover that Job is worse than everyone thinks, and the secret pain of discovering that their accusations of some hidden sin were entirely unfounded. Andersen notes that "Zophar falls into the common evangelistic error of applying the categories of guilt and pardon to every human problem" (*Job,* p. 158). Their rational, cause-effect theology may in the end be an intellectual idol, like the gods who have mouths but do not speak, feet but cannot walk (Ps 115:4-7). People who give their supreme loyalty to an inflexible, though manageable, theology will undoubtedly become inflexible. But those who worship the Lord, who "does whatever he pleases" (23:13; Ps 115:3), will themselves be moveable and surprising people.

Question 4. What Job needs is not a theological treatise but flesh and blood friends with empathetic hearts. Indeed, sometimes the wisest thing to say is nothing (13:5)! Talking about God to a suffering person is in itself never enough. Better, as Job well knows, to talk to God.

Question 5. As the drama unfolds, Job is not reacting as Satan had assumed. He does not now say, "I have given up my belief in the goodness of God. I will stop worshiping God. I will curse God and die." Rather, he rebels against his friends' inadequate theology—a theology that nevertheless represents the best wisdom of the day. He rebels against any "explanation" that requires him to be untruthful about himself in order to be honest with God. He rebels against inventing sins to satisfy his confessors. He rebels against the idea that suffering is God's last word. He rebels against the notion that his righteousness—so deeply witnessed in his own heart, though he knows not why—is a creation of his own pride rather than a gift of God. He rebels against the silence of God, believing that God does speak, God will speak, and God will speak to him (14:15). While he once wanted to be left in peace, he will now fight his way through to a restored friendship with God.

The friends have a part to play, but not what they intended. Their judging spirits initially drive Job to break the downward spiral of despair (chapter 3) in his fascination with the idea of his own death. Further, their moralistic theology compels him to justify himself, not in the improper sense of establishing one's own righteousness apart from relationship to God on the basis of performance and religious activity, but rather in the biblical sense of the attributed, given righteousness of those who "fear God and shun evil" (1:8). This is also the New Testament sense, where those who have faith in the grace of Jesus Christ and his sufficient work on the cross (Gal 2:15-21) are justified even while being sinners.

Question 6. It is not entirely clear what "two things" Job wants (13:20)! In the context Job is asking for several things: Job asks for the situation in which he can speak freely with God and bring his case forward. His intent is not merely "to argue his case" (13:3) in order to win his suit but, as the Hebrew word suggests, to reconcile the offended party by sorting out the misunderstanding. The word is used in this sense in Isaiah 1:18. As it is, Job feels intimidated and overpowered by his suffering and by God's awesome power. Job's God is so much bigger than the puny little god of Eliphaz, Bildad and Zophar, a god small enough to fit in the human brain. But Job also wants God to find something wrong with him—if he can! Most of all, he wants God to stop hiding from him and treating him as an enemy (13:24-28).

Question 7. As the passage in 14:1-6 indicates, Job thinks that one human life is too pitiful to be worth God's persistent *negative* attention. There seems to be more hope for a tree, which at least can be resuscitated into life. But whether there is any hope beyond the grave for a human being is indeed an issue (14:14) we will take up in the next question.

Question 8. The familiar and loved translation of 13:15—"Though he slay me, yet will I trust in him" (KJV)—has been widely abandoned. But, as Francis Andersen shows (*Job*, p. 166), both on textual and contextual grounds the reading of the KJV, substantially used in the NIV, should be kept.

Job is expressing the strongest confidence in both God's justice and Job's innocence. Further, he is convinced that there is a hope worth considering beyond the grave. In spite of the attempts of some scholars to prove the opposite, the text suggests that Job is "playing" with the idea of life after death, first by considering the power of a tree to be rejuvenated (14:7-9)—unlike the dried lake that is never rejuvenated (14:11-12)—and second by his daring thought that after his service is rendered (presumably in the place of the dead) he will be renewed (14:14). Job considers that if God will long for his creature and will be sorry for killing Job, God will have to find some way of covering Job's sin (14:16-17).

The Old Testament hope of continuing personal existence after death was a distinctive feature of the faith of Israel. In continuity with the Old Testament Paul proclaims that the future of the Christian person is a "spiritual body" (1 Cor 15:44) like that of Jesus—a full human existence expressed bodily. This much we share with Job. But the Christian hope is invigorated by the fact that, with the coming of Jesus, the kingdom has *already* come, though not yet fully. So we taste the powers of the age to come. Even death has lost its sting. We do not have resurrection life fully now—contrary to what some Corinthians were saying—but we do not go down to the grave, as Job contemplated, uncertain about the other side or unable to live now in the light of that glorious future. Job lived with a hope that was essentially "not yet," but in Christ we live with the tension of "now" and "not yet."

Questions 9-10. Sometimes our attempt to defend God turns out to be a disservice to God, as Job pointed out in the case of his friends (13:7). He challenges them about showing God partial, presumably by whitewashing God, by covering up the enormity of what God has allowed or caused! Job's apologetic is crucial for our own (and others') journey of faith. Job proposes that in defending God we run the risk of deceit—covering up God's apparent injustices. In Job's refusal to defend God—a rebellion of sorts, but a rebellion in faith—Job offers by example the final apologetic for God—speaking with him oneself. "But I desire to speak to the Almighty and to argue my case with God" (13:3).

Job is being tested. It is essential that he does not know why. He must ask why. He must test and reject all the answers attempted by men. In the end he will find satisfaction in what God himself tells him. (Andersen, *Job,* p. 125)

Study 6. Our Heavenly Guarantor. Job 16:1—17:3; 19:23-27.

Purpose: To learn about the grounds upon which a person can be confident that God is *for* them.

Question 1. The intention of this question is to explore the experience of certainty in general terms, to get people thinking about what they know they can count on, not necessarily to explore spiritual certainty.

Question 2. The great moments of faith-discovery in this book, of which this chapter contains one, shine all the more brightly against the dark backdrop of Job's suffering. Job piles image upon image of God's negative behavior toward him. He is a ferocious beast (16:9), a traitor (16:11), a wrestler (16:12), an archer (16:12-13), a swordsman (16:13-14) (Andersen, *Job,* p. 180).

Verse 10 is an obvious parallel to the suffering servant of Isaiah 50:6; 53:3: it is God who turns Job over to evil men (his friends) for purposes unknown to the servant but ultimately for God's glory and the accomplishment of God's purpose. Modern persons might be more comfortable to say that "it happened" without direct reference to God's agency. That might make explanation easier, but it would lead to a reduced God and reduced faith. Andersen notes that the description of Job's suffering at the hand of God does not include any indication that Job fought back, admitted that his punishment was well-deserved, or judged that God could be placated through a sacrifice (*Job*, p. 182). He sits in the dust in sackcloth, but not because he is penitent. He is grieving, but not repentant—not yet.

Question 3. In spite of his friends' accusations Job is convinced he comes to God with clean hands (11:13-15), partly because he has not cursed his companions.

Question 4. As with the Redeemer or Vindicator of 19:25, the identity of the "witness in heaven" (16:19) is somewhat uncertain. The difficulty is further complicated by the fact that the witness/intercessor pleads on behalf of God and Job at the same time. But as H. H. Rowley asserts, "It is to God that shed blood cries, and the psychological penetration of the struggle between two conceptions of God in Job's mind is greater than trust in a second heavenly figure" (*The Book of Job*, p. 121). What is certain is that Job can find a defense in heaven. "With that unresolved tension between the God of his past experience, and the God of his present experience he appeals to God against himself, and proclaims his faith that the God he has known is still his Witness in heaven against the God who so torments him" (Ibid., p. 116).

What Job cannot envision, and what constitutes the breathtaking message of the New Testament, is that God should provide within his own loving Trinity the means of reconciling his creature to himself, supplying in himself the intercession to himself which no human being is fit to offer, doing for his creature what only God can. The ultimate answer to the unresolved tension in Job's faith is the full Trinitarian revelation of God in Jesus Christ through the Spirit. But even that must be held as mystery and not as a manageable doctrine about a God who can be fully defined in mental terms.

Question 5. Job's question is profound: Who else can put up security for our lives? If we cannot control our circumstances, the principalities and powers around us, or other human beings with similar powers to ourselves, it will take a heavenly guarantor to secure our future. Just as a more affluent, powerful person will pledge his superior assets on behalf of a weaker one, so Job dares to ask God to act as his guarantor. Already he has stumbled on a heavenly friend, intercessor and witness. But now he asks God to defend him against God! To give to God what God requires. Which is exactly what God in Christ did, the One in whom all the promises of God find their yes (2 Cor 1:20).

Question 6. The acknowledged climax of the whole book is the well-known affirmation "I know that my Redeemer lives" (19:25)—an assertion all the more audacious because it comes in the context of feeling betrayed by friends and devastated by God. Many scholars question this verse and the ones following. But, in spite of the textual difficulties, the main points are wonderfully clear: (1) Job is so certain of his innocence that he will commit to writing a record of his life. (2) He will see God (three times mentioned)—something more wonderful than hearing his voice. (3) He will see God in the flesh as a real human being. (4) His Redeemer is God himself, thus resolving a notch farther the tension noted in the comments on question 5. (5) God the Redeemer will act on Job's behalf. There is enough here to warm the cockles of the heart and to evoke faith in the heart of the most beleaguered saint. What is not so certain is whether Job will see God after he has died (and has been resurrected) or before. Most probably it is the former, for reasons which Andersen outlines (*Job*, p. 194).

Question 7. The idea of a Redeemer comes from the Hebrew understanding of the solidarity of the family. The redeemer or kinsman is a brother, father or cousin who is involved in everything one does, sharing guilt or avenging an enemy. Scriptural examples abound (Num 5:8; Deut 25:5; Ruth 3:9; 2 Sam 21). That God himself should become Job's nearest relative and vindicate him forever—on whichever side of the grave he might be—is surely the highest point of revelation in this book, and can be rightly called "The Gospel According to Job." It will take the New Testament to fully develop what that Redeemer must do—taking our place, suffering for us, defending our integrity and making us a son or daughter in God's family.

Question 8. Hope and faith belong together, as the frequent mention of "faith, hope and love" in the New Testament attests. Hope is not mere human wishing (as is suggested by our normal use of "hope" in sentences like "I hope to see you tomorrow"). Hope is based on the promises of God, on the character of God, on the record of God's deeds in history. But this hope which saves us is not hope based on what is seen (Rom 8:24), that is, based on verifiable evidence that is convincing without the exercise of faith. Therefore, Paul says we wait for it patiently—as Job did—experiencing the pleading of the Spirit's intercession in our hearts (Rom 8:26-27) and responding wholeheartedly to all that we know of God. In this way the basis of Job's and our hope is like the resurrection of Jesus, which was not a self-evident fact that convinced friend and enemy against their wills and without faith. Instead, as Jesus prophesied, the resurrection would only convince people who were already obeying the word they already had from God (Lk 16:31). Job is a case in point. He was ready to receive this hope because he was acting on what he already knew about God, especially his hunch that God wanted to be his friend.

Study 7. The Problem of Pain. Job 20:1-19; 21:1-16.

Purpose: To explore the potential and the limitations of a rational explanation for the problem of suffering.

Question 3. After reflecting on Job's retort, which Zophar considers to be an insult, Zophar elaborates on his view that the success of the wicked is both brief and self-destructive (v. 15). The death of the wicked will be swift (v. 8) and premature (v. 11).

Question 4. Zophar moves a little closer to Job's position, newly gained in the last study, that the final solution for the justice of God in the affairs of the world may not be found on this side of the grave. Zophar is discovering "that confidence in God's justice is not based on observation, but is a matter of trust and hope" (Andersen, *Job*, p. 196).

Question 5. Zophar still has no place in his theology for the suffering of the righteous and the innocent. Zophar and his friends operate on the assumption that sin produces suffering and that suffering proves sin.

Question 6. Job's speech in chapter 21 is the least prayerful (it is directed to the friends) and the most dialogical (it answers point by point the arguments of his friends, unlike his other speeches). For example, Eliphaz earlier stated that Job's tent would be safe if he were righteous (5:24); Job, now homeless, observes that the houses or tents of the wicked are secure (21:9). Bildad maintained that the wicked die childless (18:19); Job, having lost all his family, observes that the wicked have large, happy families (21:11). Zophar has just affirmed that the wicked die prematurely (20:11); Job, looking with both fear and fascination at his own imminent death, observes that the wicked live long and seem to get healthier as the years go by (21:7)! Some of the statements made by Job in this passage—obviously the opposite of what Job believes—are apparently quotations from his friends (v. 19). In the end (21:34) Job rejects their consolation as nonsense that, in face of reality, is blatantly false.

Job has moved beyond contemplating his own experience of unjust suffering to the more general problem: why there seems to be no correspondence between doing good and being rewarded, and doing evil and being punished. In chapter 24—worth being studied in this connection—Job takes up the case for the whole of suffering and crucified humanity. Realizing that his own situation is the same as that of the poor, the powerless and the dispossessed, he considers that the problem of pain is not only personal (to people like himself) but constitutional (in the way the world is run).

Speaking to this, Gustavo Gutiérrez notes that the West has not had a theology of the evil of misfortune, the evil suffered by the innocent. What liberation theology might contribute—in spite of its limitations—is the attempt to account for "widespread, objective evil that entails no fault in the sufferer" (*On Job,* p. xv). So Job's cry is not only on his own behalf but on behalf of the needs of his neighbor. Gutiérrez notes that this represents a shift in Job's spirituality since "he sees now that this poverty and abandonment are not something fated but caused by the wicked, who nonetheless live serene and satisfied lives" (p. 32).

The cruel wretchedness of the poor and the indictment of the powerful in chapter 24 are the most radical in the Bible, though this theme is taken up elsewhere (Jer 22:13-17; Amos 5:11-12; Mic 2:9). In 21:14 Job notes that it is the same ones who tell God, "Leave us alone. We have no desire to know your ways" that are the rich and prosperous. However, Gutiérrez observes that the final answer to the injustice of the world and the exploitation of the nameless poor is found in God's speech in the whirlwind (Job 38—41). See the note for question 9.

Question 8. Known only to the reader is that the sufferings were brought on at the instigation of Satan. This, however, does not explain Job's suffering. In fact Satan never appears again in the book and is never cited by Job, the friends or God as the source of human suffering. Further, and still unknown to Job, there are passages in the Bible that postpone resolving the questions about how God is managing the world until the end of history—and beyond. Job is not ready for a full eschatological (end-times) answer yet. But Job has made significant progress in his journey.

Job has stopped requiring everything to be worked out this side of the grave.

He has a witness in heaven (16:19) and now believes he will see his Redeemer-Kinsman in a real human existence, though probably after he has died. He will sink again into despair, weary of his friends' pestering preaching and wondering about his own unrelieved suffering. But he now knows that the "answer" to the problem of pain is more than theological; it involves relationship with a caring God who, in the end, will not turn his back on him.

One of the answers Job will eventually test, initially raised by Eliphaz (5:17) but expounded later by the young man Elihu (36:10), is that suffering is a chastening of God for our moral and spiritual improvement. While this theme is suggested elsewhere in the Bible (Ps 94:12; Prov 3:11; Heb 12:5), it falls short of a full answer to Job's (or anyone else's) suffering and is not mentioned by God in the whirlwind speeches. Abraham's test (Gen 22), a case in point, is rightly considered a miniature book of Job (Andersen, *Job*, p. 125). Abraham's suffering was initiated by God but was neither a punishment for his sins nor a corrective measure for his improvement. Yet it was an experience which enlarged his faith in God and changed his life forever. In the same vein Andersen notes that the full biblical answer to the problem of pain is that God can and does actually transform evil into good "so that in retrospect (but only in retrospect!) it is seen to have actually been good, without diminishing in the least the awful actuality of the evil it was at the time" (ibid., p. 69). The final answer given in the Bible to the problem of pain is the cross of Jesus where God finally and completely transforms evil into good and personally as a suffering God bears the pain of his own creature redemptively.

Question 9. Speaking of Job's response to God's final "answer" to the problem of pain given in the whirlwind speech, Gustavo Gutierrez says: "The truth [Job] has grasped and that has lifted him to the level of contemplation is that justice alone does not have the final say about how we are to speak of God. Only when we have come to realize that God's love is freely bestowed do we enter fully and definitely into the presence of the God of faith" (*On Job*, p. 87). God's love does not operate in a world of cause and effect, but in freedom and gratuitiveness.

Zophar wants a theology that makes the sun shine only on the righteous. Job sees the wicked receiving God's blessing and the righteous receiving pain. He is not convinced that Zophar's mechanical cause-effect theology is right, and he is exploring through prayer an alternative. Eventually, he will be ready to declare that God gives generously without respect to the worthiness of the recipient. The drama started with Satan's question "Does Job fear God for nothing?" Now the drama is moving to a deeper, though related, question: "Does God give his love and blessing for nothing?" Put in other words, the fundamental question of the book may be framed, "Is God so good that he can be loved simply for himself and not for his gifts?" but that question is explored in the context of the question "Are human beings so loved by God that God will care for them regardless of their behavior and worthiness?"

Question 10. This final question is probed helpfully in *Search the Scriptures*: "In this second cycle Job's friends, gaining no victory, utter threats. Is defeated conservatism bound to take refuge in acid predictions of gloom? Had Job something to teach them if only they were willing to listen?" (Alan M. Stibbs, ed., rev. ed. [InterVarsity

Press, 1969], p. 227).

Study 8. The Silence of God. Job 23.

Purpose: To explore the silence of God as a loving invitation to honest prayer and communion.

Questions 2-3. Job's friends want Job to repent of his sins. Job's problem is this: he admits he is a sinner (19:4) but he cannot account for his suffering by errors on his part.

Job wants to present his case personally to God. Given the opportunity, he believes he could convince God that he is truly righteous (v. 4)—the very thing God already knows, though this fact is unknown to Job (1:8)! Earlier he cringed at the thought of a face-to-face confrontation. Now he desires such a meeting, not only because his pilgrimage has led him to the conviction that he has a friend and relative in heaven, but also because he now wants God even more than he wants answers to his questions. On the one hand this seems to be the height of self-righteousness, especially when one realizes that the acceptance he seeks is not the pardon of a guilty man by grace but the acquittal of a righteous man by law (Andersen, *Job,* p. 209). On the other hand this hunger for justification seems entirely in the mainstream of true biblical spirituality.

Job feared God and shunned evil even by the Lord's own assessment (1:8). Job could point, as he later does, to his stunning record positively in chapter 29 (rejoicing in the light of God's presence and loving the poor and powerless) and negatively in chapter 31 (shunning the full catalogue of sins of spirit, mind and body). This is no mere salvation by works but is entirely in line with the Pauline doctrine of justification by faith, a principle to which both the law and prophets point (Rom 3:21). The fear of God, as the wisdom poem (28:1-28) indicates, is a holy marriage of reverence for God and morality in life (28:28). In New Testament terms it is faith active in love. So Job has every reason to desire a meeting with God. Put differently, having already experienced the judgment of his friends, he now has less fear of the judgment of God. Albert Camus spoke to this with great depth:

> Believe me, religions are on the wrong track the moment they moralize and fulminate commandments. God is not needed to create guilt or to punish. Our fellow men suffice, aided by ourselves. You were speaking of the Last Judgement. . . . I shall wait for it resolutely, for I have known what is worse, the judgement of men. For them, no extenuating circumstances; even the good intention is ascribed to crime. (As quoted in Robert A. Raines, *Creative Brooding* [Macmillan (US), 1966], p. 51.)

Questions 4-5. Verses 8 and 9 tell us that Job does not know where to go to find God. But there is a deeper reason for God's apparent unavailability. Just as Jesus delayed going to Bethany when he heard of Lazarus's illness (Jn 11:5-6) because of his love for him, so God withholds the full experience of his presence for reasons only partly known to us. John White notes that "we confuse intimacy with its counterfeit, familiarity. Intimacy is what we want but familiarity is all we achieve. Intimacy is dangerous, a knowing and a being known deeply and profoundly".

(*Daring to Draw Near* [InterVarsity Press (US), 1977], p. 100).

Question 6. Blaise Pascal said that to search for God is to know that you have already been found by him! So the true pilgrim speaks more of being known *by* God (Ps 139:1; Gal 4:9) than of knowing God. That indeed is Job's hope: God knows him better than his friends do!

Questions 7-8. Andersen notes that Job holds together two opposites: the consciousness of an intimate personal relationship with God by walking in God's ways (lining his life up with God's commands and wisdom, v. 11) and a vivid awareness that he is currently being denied fellowship with God (*Job*, p. 209). So Job has lived by fearing God and shunning evil (the Old Testament equivalent of living by Spirit and Word) even without the attending confirmation of the nearness of God. But that obedience is itself a prayer, a prayer that will eventually be answered in a way chosen by God. Simone Weil spoke to this: "For us, this obedience in relation to God is what the transparency of a window pane is in relation to light. As soon as we feel this obedience with our whole being, we see God" (*Waiting on God*, [Collins, 1950], p. 89.) In other words God is not entirely silent since he has given us wisdom and Scripture. His seeming silence and our waiting are the fertile ground for faith. When and if God so chooses, faith will become sight, if not on this side of the grave, at least on the other.

Question 9. The Hebrew text here has been variously interpreted, but it seems best to understand *way* in verse 10 not as Job's way but God's way taken by Job (Andersen, *Job*, p. 210): "God knows his way with me."

Job is coming to the place where he could live without an answer for his suffering because he is convinced that God knows that he is walking in the steps of the Lord (v. 11). Therefore the test he is undergoing is not the purification process of removing the dross, but the testing to prove that Job himself is pure gold in God's sight—the very thing Job has maintained from the start! This is not self-righteousness but the boldness of true faith. Job is an Old Testament prototype of the true gospel believer who dares to come to God just as he is because—as we learn in the New Testament—of an imputed, given righteousness through faith in God's Son and our Messiah, Jesus.

Questions 10-11. Compared with the puny God of Job's friends, Job's God is completely unmanageable: "He does whatever he pleases." Job's God cannot be tamed (see 12:13-25), and therefore cannot be manipulated into giving justice. That is both Job's problem and his hope. As we will soon see when God reveals himself to Job in the whirlwind (chapters 38—41), Job's final "answer" is found in the revelation of a God so great that the only appropriate response is worship. John White says, "The problem of suffering remains incompletely solved in the book, but for Job it no longer existed. It is not just that his fortunes were restored again. A greater richness had come into his life, the richness a man knows when he treasures the majesty and glory of God" (*Daring*, p. 109).

Study 9. Songs in the Night. Job 35; 36:13-16.

Purpose: To show the futility of trying to explain specific situations in people's lives by appealing to general theological principles.

Questions 2-3. The four speeches of Elihu (32:1—37:24) are sometimes thought to add nothing to the discussion. Job does not even respond to Elihu. God doesn't mention Elihu when he comments on the ministry of the friends (42:7). But Elihu does add something to the discussion, and his speeches form an important transition from the defiant Job to the God who speaks in the storm.

It is the wicked, Job says, who ask, "What would we gain by praying to him?" (21:15). Unknown to both Job and Elihu, Satan asked this question as well (1:9-10). So Elihu infers that this is what is bothering Job, while, all along, Job's deepest concern is not with what he gets out of being righteous but what has happened to his relationship with God. Elihu misses this, because he is determined to uphold the honor and justice of God. Elihu believes that human righteousness does not affect God at all (v. 7). God, in this man's view, is neither delighted with a good man nor grieved with an evil man, since God is an impartial administrator (34:19). In so speaking of God he believes he is defending God's honor, but in fact he is defending his own theology.

Question 4. Elihu's God is distant and impartial—not affected by human action, whether good or evil. The result of such a view is human indifference. Rational answers to the problem of pain will always leave the heart cold. That Elihu's theology is an expression of his own cold heart is indicated by the curse he calls down on Job: "Oh, that Job might be tested to the utmost for answering like a wicked man!" (34:36).

Question 6. This question *was* asked by Job, over and again. It was Job's obsession. More than anything—even any *thing*—Job wanted God, God's fellowship, God's Word, God's approval, God's presence.

The range of answers supplied by the friends are similar to those heard today: "not enough faith," "unconfessed sin" (v. 12), "you are not praying right" (v. 16). Elihu, and his modern counterparts, can deal with unanswered prayer with a handy formula: God answers the righteous who pray correctly; God judges the wicked. How could God answer Job's prayers that are so ignorant (v. 16)? For Elihu there is no mystery to God's work. Like the three other friends, he has God well managed. But he is unable to "manage" Job's predicament any better than his older friends. Job, in contrast, "lives in the suspense of faith, praying without guarantees" (Andersen, *Job,* p. 258).

Question 7. Elihu does bring an important emphasis—he talks about what we can learn from suffering. It is not entirely absent from the previous speeches but now is drawn out more explicitly. If, as C. S. Lewis once observed, God whispers to us in our pleasures, he shouts at us in our pain. Elihu says something similar in the passage next to be studied: "he speaks to them in their affliction" (36:15). This may relate to Elihu's most beautiful contribution to the discussion, his reference to God giving us "songs in the night" (35:10)—surely a hint of God's graciousness in an otherwise cheerless lecture.

Question 9. The search for an answer to Job's suffering by finding a sufficient cause has failed. Elihu's fourth speech (36:1—37:24) makes an important transition from cause-effect theology to mystery. Elihu now moves in the direction God will take up—so much more redemptively—when God finally speaks: the direction of the gratuitousness of God. God does not despise people (36:5-12). Indeed he uses trouble to train people in righteousness, a use which makes even adversity somewhat sweet (v. 15), so sweet that they can hear or sing songs in the night (a metaphor of God's comfort in the most cheerless time). While it is true that the person who refuses to pray when in trouble comes to a shameful and untimely end (36:13-14), God is actually wooing people in affliction to himself. Elihu uses the Hebrew expression which would be used by a young man pleading for the heart of his beloved. Though Elihu makes a positive contribution to the discussion, it pales before the direct revelation of God to Job which will follow.

Study 10. God in the Storm. Job 38:1-11, 31-41; 40:1-5

Purpose: To understand God's response to Job—knowing God is more important than getting answers to our moral dilemmas.

Questions 2-3. The range of creatures noted by God in chapters 38 and 39 is a significant sample: earth (vv. 38:4-7), sea (vv. 8-11), morning (vv. 12-15), the underworld (vv. 16-18), light (vv. 19-21), snow (vv. 22-23), storm (vv. 24-27), rain (vv. 28-30), the constellations (vv. 31-33), clouds (vv. 34-38), the lion (vv. 39-40), ravens (v. 41), the ibex (39:1-4), the wild ass (vv. 5-8), the wild ox (vv. 9-12), the ostrich (vv. 13-18), the horse (vv. 19-25), the hawk (v. 26), the eagle (vv. 27-30).

God's deluge of questions relating to these creatures does not seem to have anything to do with why Job has suffered so severely. But to begin with, the use of questions by God is significant. They are, as Andersen notes, not a way of making a pronouncement but are "invitations, suggestions about discoveries he will make as he tries to find his own answers" (*Job,* p. 269). They are educative in the true sense—not meant to humiliate Job but to call him to learn in God's schoolroom, the world. The world, Job will be led to see, is not, as moderns so proudly assume, created for humankind, for our pleasure and exploitation. Just the reverse: we were made *for* the world—to take care of it (Gen 2:5, 15). But even more surprising, the world was, we now realize, made for God's glory and pleasure, as witnessed by God's reminder that God makes grass and flowers to grow and flourish on the distant moors "where no man lives" (38:26). By a barrage of carefully crafted questions God brings Job to the place of knowing that he is not the creator of the world. He wasn't even around at the time!

Questions 4-5. God emphasizes what Job cannot do, rather than what he can do as an awesome God-imaging creature. In another section of the poem, God reminds Job that God makes rain fall and grass grow in places where no human will ever tread. We might have appreciated hearing how humankind can tame certain animals. God wants us to know that only God can make a wild donkey (39:5-8).

God's obvious enjoyment of his own creation is one of the subtle messages of the book. Not so subtle is the fact that Job will get along with himself better if he is rightly related *both* to the Creator and the creation, a principle largely lost in modern life, which encourages relationship either to the creation (parts of the environmental movement) or to the Creator (the spirituality movement). These beautiful poems about goats and ostriches, constellations and sea monsters (probably the crocodile) are right on target: it is as a man in the world among other creatures that Job will find answers to his questions, and if not, the capacity to live with joy when his questions remain unanswered.

Question 6. The passage begins with a misunderstood phrase: "Who is this that darkens my counsel?" (v. 2). "Counsel" usually refers to the plan and providence of God, something which God will declare Job spoke well about (42:8). The meaning is apparently that Job is in the dark having received the advice ("knowledge") dispensed by the wise men around him (his friends). Now God will bring his own light to Job's problem (Andersen, *Job,* pp. 273-74). Presumably Job will draw some conclusions about his creatureliness: he did not exist from the beginning of time; he cannot be everywhere at once; he cannot endow the heart with wisdom (v. 36) or discharge lightning bolts; he has not yet been through the death experience (v. 17). All of this is designed to help Job put his problems into perspective. He is, after all, a creature, not God. In spite of God's progressive whittling of Job down to size, there is no suggestion that God despises Job. Just the reverse. God invites Job to stand up like a man (38:3) and enter into dialogue with God. Francis Andersen notes:

> There is a kindly playfulness in the Lord's speeches which is quite relaxing. Their aim is not to crush Job with an awareness of his minuteness contrasted with the limitless power of God, not to mock him when he puts his tiny mind beside God's vast intellect. On the contrary, the mere fact that God converses with him gives him a dignity above all the birds and beasts, assuring him that it is a splendid thing to be a man. (*Job,* p. 271.)

Question 7. It important to catch the tone of the Lord's point. He is not trying to force Job to capitulate to God's superior wisdom. "Answer" does not imply "answering back" but something more friendly, indeed something ironical. If Job understands any of the matters above better than God himself, then God would be willing to learn from Job (Andersen, *Job,* p. 285)!

Question 8. The response of clapping hands over the mouth has been previously noted. In 21:5, responding to the friends' tirade, Job asked his friends to look on him with astonishment and clap their hands over their mouths to stem the tide of their inappropriate speech. Job recalls that before he was devastated by God, the chief men in the village would show their respect for Job by refraining from speaking—all the more unusual coming from the nobles (29:9). Now it is Job's turn. Job has no answer to God's questions.

Questions 9-10. Job has not necessarily submitted and repented (contrary to what some commentators suggest). He is respectfully silent, but the matter is not over. Apparently, the Lord sees it this way because he takes up his speech a second time. Not every complaint is a revolt. And blind, unthinking submission is not the hallmark of faith. But in every complaint there will be elements of non-faith which, in the context of God's loving ministry, can be brought into harmony with his glory and purpose.

Jean-Pierre De Caussaude proposes: "To find contentment in the present moment is to relish and adore the divine will in the succession of all the things to be done and suffered which make up the duty to the present moment" (*The Sacrament of the Present Moment*, trans. Kitty Muggeridge [Glasgow: Collins, 1981], p. 84). Job is not there yet—and should not be rushed into a compliant grudging submission as an alternative to loving faith.

Job wanted an audience to demonstrate in what an exemplary way he has run his life. What he got was a lecture on how well God runs the world. Job wanted deliverance from his judge (23:7). God speaks about how much he enjoys being judge. Job wanted God to look favorably on him—one special creature from the land of Uz. What Job got was an invitation to appreciate two of God's most splendid and uncontrollable creatures: the hippopotamus (40:15-24) and the crocodile (41:1-34). Job wanted to prove his innocence. God proved Job's littleness. Job wanted an intimate conversation with his friend in heaven (29:4). God gave him poetry and some hymns of praise.

Study 11. The Joy of Repentance. Job 40:6-14; 42:1-6.

Purpose: To deepen our understanding and experience of repentance as a positive and life-giving posture.

Question 2. In 40:4-5 Job has nothing to say (the hand clapped over the mouth), but he has not yet admitted his sin. And God's resumption into a second speech is a further loving ministry to bring Job to peace with God, himself and the entire created order. Job is not defiant but still has not got the point, a point which God probes both by direct questioning (vv. 6-14) and indirect analogies (40:7—41:34). Were Job already repentant and submissive God could get on with others matters. Martin Buber said that real self-knowledge leads a person either to self-destruction or to rebirth (as quoted in Raines, *Creative Brooding*, p. 14). It is a perilous moment.

Questions 3-4. Without intending to, Job has been discrediting and condemning God by insisting that his own view of the moral structure of the world is the right one. By Job's view God is not living up to his own highest morality: he lets the wicked get off scot-free and allows the righteous (like himself) to go through hell on earth. Without saying so, he is asserting that if God is God, he is not good. If he were good he would approve of Job's righteousness against the condemning sneer of his friends. So Job refuses to repent of sins—the sins dreamed up by his friends to "justify" his obvious experience of God's punishments. *And in this Job was right!* Indeed he never is required by God to repent of the friends' "list." But while he need not repent of sins, he must get a deeper grasp of sin—the root problem. To do this God must expand his horizons so he can repent willingly and gladly rather than reluctantly and dismally.

Question 5. Verses 7-14 are the heart of the Lord's reply to Job and are significantly placed between the two nature speeches. The problem of putting God in the wrong in order to prove Job in the right is placed in a much larger moral context. In these verses Job is reminded that only if Job had the right of humbling the proud and crushing the evil—the right to exercise God's judgment—could God allow Job to vindicate himself (vv. 11-14). Some help in understanding this is given by knowing how justice worked in Hebrew society. The judge gave the verdict, passed sentence and secured the right of the injured party. "It was only indirectly, in connection with restoring things to rights, that wrongdoers were punished" (Andersen, *Job*, p. 286).

What God wants Job to admit is this: as a creature he does not have the ability to administer his own justice or to vindicate himself. God's references to his own power in creation is fundamental to this. The two nature poems in 40:15—41:34 (the behemoth is possibly the hippopotamus and the leviathan is possibly the crocodile) indicate two creatures that a human being would find impossible to tame, a fact significant to Job's underlying problem. Verse 9 says, "Do you have an arm like God's?" To take over the moral administration of the universe Job would have to be as powerful as God. Job knows this, but he has not been able, thus far, to accept the Lord's administration of the world without fretting, without complaining, without reservation. He is struggling to let God be God, and this brings us to the heart of his repentance.

Question 7. With considerable depth Francis Andersen comments on the theology of the book at this point.

> There is a rebuke in [this book] for any person who, by complaining about particular events in his life, he could propose to God better ways of running the universe than those God currently uses. Men are eager to use force to combat evil and in their impatience they wish God would do the same more often. But by such destructive acts men do and become evil. To behave as God suggests in 40:8-14, Job would not only usurp the role of God, he would become another Satan. Only God can destroy creatively. Only God can transmute evil into good. As Creator, responsible for all that happens in His world, He is able to make everything (good and bad) work together into good. The debate has been elevated to a different level. The reality of God's goodness lies beyond justice. That is why the categories of guilt and punishment, true and terrible though they are can only view human suffering as a consequence of sin, not as an occasion of grace. (*Job,* pp. 287-88.)

Job has an expanded view of the world, seeing himself as a creature simultaneously relating to the Creator and other creatures. God's power and glory throb through it all. He cannot control God, not even in his theology. Job now has moved from "hear-say" evidence for God to firsthand encounter—"seeing" God (42:5) as few other saints have. He knows his Redeemer lives (19:25). He has unrestrained admiration for God (42:2). What he confesses at this point is not his list of sins but the greatness of God.

Question 8. Getting to the heart of Job's repentance is crucial, not only for a clear understanding of how the story really ends, but for our own relationship with God. It is quite apparent that Job never capitulates to his friends' spiritual direction to repent of his sins. It would be dishonest so to do, and God does not require it.

What happens in Job's heart is more fundamental. Just as the "sins" of Romans 1:22-32 are mere symptoms (expressed in different ways in different people) of the root sin of irreverence and ingratitude (1:21), so the root of Job's problem is found in his impoverished worship of God. He needs to repent *to* reverence and gratitude.

Job cannot make himself grovel by mere introspection or by succumbing to the judgment of other creatures. Such groveling can turn out merely to be another form of self-help "works" with no faith in it. It might even be the cloak of pride turned inside out. Instead of being repentance it might be remorse, shame or even false guilt. True repentance is not worked up from below but inspired from above. And Job cannot repent until he meets God. When he does meet God he *wants* to repent, not of some puny list of things done that should not have been done, or things not done that should have been (he argues just the reverse in chapters 29—31). He repents of something more fundamental: of trying to be God, of pretending that he can think like God, of playing God.

Question 10. The translation "despise myself" is possibly inaccurate. "Myself" does not appear in the original Hebrew. Unquestionably Job is now a humble suppliant like Abraham (Gen 18:27), but he is not groveling in the sudden realization that his sins are almost innumerable and punishment will soon engulf him. His repentance involved self-depreciation in the deepest and healthiest sense of relinquishing a godlike presumption. His repentance involved welcoming his status as a creature, though never as a "mere" creature. Speaking to the distinction between healthy repentance and unhealthy self-disgust, John White says, "He is at peace who has seen himself appropriately placed in the total scheme of things" (*Daring*, p. 106).

Study 12. Is Faith Always Worthwhile? Job 42:7-17.

Purpose: To explore the message of Job as it relates to disinterested faith—faith *for* the love of God.

Questions 2-3. One of the strangest reversals of the book is God's assessment of the situation. The friends delivered conservative orthodox theology to the rebellious Job—and were judged for not speaking correctly about God. Job storms heaven with his prayers—vacillating between wanting an audience with God to prove his innocence and fearing that if he ever got such an audience he would be tongue-tied in terror—and God says Job spoke correctly!

Earlier we noted that while the friends spoke *about* God, Job spoke *to* God (in prayer). This is a crucial point. Job's "full encounter with his God came by way of complaint, bewilderment, and confrontation" (Gutiérrez, *On Job,* p. 55), but he got to God in the end because he prayed. In his prayer and desire to be with God, Job revealed his right belief in God. His friends had God theologically managed, but their God was a distant god of sterile rationalism. They represented the religious wisdom of Job's day.

Question 5. The book is full of ironies, some of which have already been discovered. Here is another: The friends who came to "comfort" Job in his misery (but failed to do so) are now in need of Job's patronage. It is surely one more indication of Job's "disinterested" faith, now deepened by his discovery of the free love of God given to good and evil, that he prays for his former accusers. "My servant Job will pray for you, and I will accept his prayer" (42:8).

Questions 7-8. Significantly, the restoration of his fortunes is not timed with his repentance but with his intercession for his friends. There is not a shred of evidence that the author of Job has slipped back, as some allege, into a crude theology of rewards and punishments—the very thing this book transcends in its central message. Early in the book, when Job first experienced excruciating loss, he blessed God (1:21) instead of cursing him, thus proving Satan wrong at least in the first test. Job does not need material prosperity to sustain his trust in God. After each trial, Job persists in his integrity. His faith is not inspired by the hope of material reward. As Gutiérrez notes, "It is thus made clear from the outset that gratuitiveness is a main characteristic of authentic faith in God" (*On Job,* p. 54). The gifts of God at the end—cattle, sons and daughters—were "gestures of grace, not rewards for virtue" (Andersen, *Job,* p. 294).

Question 10. Rational answers to the problem of pain have little place in the ministry to a suffering person asking, Why? What people need is friends, and listening friends at that! The ultimate question is not Why? but Who? The reason some people come to faith in God, or remain so, seems to have little to do with life, or their experience of life. Some who go through hard times—with no explanation—believe all the more; others become bitter. The difference has something to do with prayer and the God to whom they believe they are praying. Job is bitter against life but not bitter against God. He attributes all his suffering to God (even though the book does not) and yet he still cries out to God and wants God. Does Job fear God for his own salvation or justification? No, he does not think he is justified by God even though he feels that he is innocent, certainly innocent of all that his friends accuse him of. Faith in God is not *for* anything, not even for salvation, certainly not for earthly benefits. It is for God.

Question 11. In the last study we saw that Job had to repent of attempting to understand everything. "The truth that he has grasped and that has lifted him to the level of contemplation is that justice alone does not have the final say about how we are to speak of God. Only when we have come to realize that God's love is freely bestowed do we enter fully and definitively into the presence of the God of faith" (Gutiérrez, *On Job,* p. 87). Job must live with mystery.

In abandoning now even his need for an "explanation," Job truly believes, more than ever before, in an utterly disinterested way—for nothing.

It is one of the many excellences of the book that Job is brought to contentment without ever knowing all the facts of his case. In view of the way in which the Satan brought up the matter, something had to be done to rescue Job from his slander. And the test would only work if Job did not know what it was for. God thrusts Job into an experience of dereliction to make it possible for Job to enter into a life of naked faith, to learn to love God for Himself alone. God does not seem to give this privilege to many people, for they pay a terrible price of suffering for their discoveries. But part of the discovery is to see the suffering itself as one of God's most precious gifts. To withhold the full story from Job, even after the test is over, keeps him walking by faith, not by sight. He does not say in the end, "Now I see it all." He never sees it all. He sees God (42:5). Perhaps it is better if God never tells any of us the whole of our life-story. (Andersen, *Job,* p. 270)

So, in the end, Job loves God not for the reward but because God is God. This is all the more remarkable since this ancient saint apparently did not have the benefit of the covenant community of Israel, the memories of God's mighty acts in history and the revelation of God's purpose in the prophets. His whole experience contradicted the principle of loving God for his own sake. So it might truly be said, "Next to Jesus, Job must be the greatest *believer* in the whole Bible" (Andersen, *Job,* p. 271).

R. Paul Stevens teaches at Regent College in Vancouver, British Columbia. He is also the author of the LifeBuilder Bible Studies 1 Corinthians *(coauthored with Dan Williams),* 2 Corinthians, Revelation *and* End Times.

What Should We Study Next?

A good place to start your study of Scripture would be with a book study. Many groups begin with a Gospel such as *Mark* (22 studies by Jim Hoover) or *John* (26 studies by Douglas Connelly). These guides are divided into two parts so that if 22 or 26 weeks seems like too much to do at once, the group can feel free to do half and take a break with another topic. Later you might want to come back to it. You might prefer to try a shorter letter. *Philippians* (9 studies by Donald Baker), *Ephesians* (13 studies by Andrew T. and Phyllis J. Le Peau) and *1 & 2 Timothy and Titus* (12 studies by Pete Sommer) are good options. If you want to vary your reading with an Old Testament book, consider *Ecclesiastes* (12 studies by Bill and Teresa Syrios) for a challenging and exciting study.

There are a number of interesting topical LifeBuilder studies as well. Here are some options for filling three or four quarters of a year:

Basic Discipleship
Christian Beliefs, 12 studies by Stephen D. Eyre
Christian Character, 12 studies by Andrea Sterk & Peter Scazzero
Christian Disciplines, 12 studies by Andrea Sterk & Peter Scazzero
Evangelism, 12 studies by Rebecca Pippert & Ruth Siemens

Building Community
Christian Community, 12 studies by Rob Suggs
Fruit of the Spirit, 9 studies by Hazel Offner
Spiritual Gifts, 12 studies by Charles & Anne Hummel

Character Studies
New Testament Characters, 12 studies by Carolyn Nystrom
Old Testament Characters, 12 studies by Peter Scazzero
Old Testament Kings, 12 studies by Carolyn Nystrom
Women of the Old Testament, 12 studies by Gladys Hunt

The Trinity
Meeting God, 12 studies by J. I. Packer
Meeting Jesus, 13 studies by Leighton Ford
Meeting the Spirit, 12 studies by Douglas Connelly